EXTREME
parenting

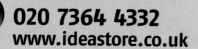

EXTREME
parenting

Parenting Your Child with a Chronic Illness

Sharon Dempsey

foreword by Hilton Davis

Jessica Kingsley Publishers
London and Philadelphia

The information offered in this book is not intended to substitute advice from health professionals. I write as a parent, drawing on my experiences and research. My hope is to assist you to be the best parent possible in difficult and challenging situations; to be an exceptional parent for your exceptional child.

First published in 2008
by Jessica Kingsley Publishers
116 Pentonville Road
London N1 9JB, UK
and
400 Market Street, Suite 400
Philadelphia, PA 19106, USA

www.jkp.com

Library of Congress Cataloging in Publication Data

Dempsey, Sharon, 1969-
  Extreme parenting : parenting your child with a chronic illness / Sharon Dempsey ; foreword by Hilton Davis. -- 1st American pbk.
    p. cm.
  Includes bibliographical references and index.
  ISBN 978-1-84310-619-7 (pb : alk. paper) 1. Children with a chronic illness--Family relationships. 2. Chronic diseases in children--Psychological aspects. 3. Children with a chronic illness--Medical care. 4. Parents of children with a chronic illness. I. Title.
  RJ380.D46 2008
  618.92--dc22

                              2007037855

British Library Cataloguing in Publication Data
A CIP catalogue record for this book is available from the British Library

ISBN 978 1 84310 619 7

Printed and bound in Great Britain by
Athenaeum Press, Gateshead, Tyne and Wear

for Owen

LONDON BOROUGH TOWER HAMLETS	
C001555120	
HJ	21/04/2008
618.92	£13.99

Contents

Acknowledgements

I am indebted to the individuals whose expertise, care and compassion was given to Owen throughout his illness. Many individuals were involved in treating Owen and caring for him and I hope I have not overlooked anyone significant to him.

To Owen's neurosurgeon Mr Richard Hatfield and his team in the University Heath Hospital in Cardiff.

To Owen's first oncologist, Dr Martin English, formerly of Llandough Hospital.

To Owen's Belfast oncologist Dr Anthony McCarthy and his team in children's haematology at Royal Belfast Hospital for Sick Children.

To the many nurses who cared for Owen: Sinead, Deirdre, Kate, Brenda – apologies if I have failed to name everyone.

To our Cardiff friends, the Autons, the Averills, the Biggs, the Shanahans and the Nant Fawr neighbours.

To the families we encountered on the haematology ward, especially the Laverys, the Martins, the Marrs, the Moriartys and the Lyles.

To Carol Burns, Owen's family support worker, and Naomi Spence, Owen's play therapist, both from Clic Sargent.

To Owen's GPs Dr Johnny Browne, Dr Paddy Sharkey, Dr Andrea Murray, Dr Ursula Mason and Dr Mark McIvor.

To Owen's pharmacist Gareth Newberry and his staff.

To Owen's teachers Hester Graham, Margaret Rolston and all the staff and pupils of St Joseph's nursery school and primary school.

To Owen's priests Father Feargal McGrady and Father Sean McCartney.

To Owen's best friends George, Robert James, Ciaran, Laurence, James, Peter, Jamie, Scott and Conall.

To our families: the Copeland and the Dempsey clans and in particular my parents Jeannie and Teddy Copeland who, in holding Owen's hand, held mine.

Thank you.

Throughout the book I have quoted the words of families who were generous in sharing with me their experiences. I have protected the anonymity of their words to enable them to speak freely.

Special thanks to those who helped in my research: Patricia, Alfie, Caroline and Michael Copeland, Debbie and Daniel Marrs, Kim McDermott and Robert James Lavery, Carmel and Cathy Lavery, Carol Burns, Dr Anthony McCarthy, Dr Arun Mathews, Professor Jane Grimson, Jennifer and Matthew Carberry, Catherine Murnin of the Child Brain Injury Trust, Gina Connor, Mo McDevitt, Finola Beattie, Dr Ursula Mason and Dr Andrea Murray. Thanks to Brenda Hoy for reading the final draft.

Preface

Every new parent is aware of the plethora of books offering advice on how to look after our children. We are instructed to follow routines to encourage 'contented' babies, to cook only organic produce, to stimulate, educate and play, all with the intention of creating happy and thriving children.

Parenting is challenging.

Some families live with additional challenges in parenting children who are chronically ill. They have the same desire to help their child reach their full potential but have added pressures of specialist care, long-term medical treatment and invasive hospital procedures.

To care for a child with a chronic illness is parenting at its most extreme. The everyday demands are heightened. Simple tasks become huge obstacles when worries and concerns threaten to overwhelm. This book is born out of the need to acknowledge the difficulties of exceptional parenting, and to offer advice and support on how to create a family dynamic that can accommodate the demands of living with chronic illness.

Extreme parenting, like an extreme sport, challenges us to find our true strengths, to push ourselves physically and emotionally. The challenges are great but so too are the rewards. Families with a child who is chronically ill are normal families thrown into the turmoil of an abnormal situation. They have everyday family demands, work and childcare issues, worries about their children's schooling, household chores, relationship or family problems and financial pressures, all of which need to be resolved within the context of caring for a child with physical, medical and emotional needs that demand time and attention.

We are all fundamentally resilient. We want to do our best for our children so we want to cope. Coping, living well, enjoying one's children and doing more than just surviving is achievable with the right information, strategies and support.

My son Owen was diagnosed with an ependymoma brain tumour at the age of two. He underwent nine hours of neurosurgery and sixteen months of intensive chemotherapy. When his tumour recurred and spread to his spine, he had further chemotherapy and radiotherapy. Owen died at the age of six. His life, although short, was full. He taught me how to look illness face on and to make every moment count. No matter how ill he felt or how much pain he suffered, he still wanted to live and be a part of this world. I have let his example guide me through the dark days without him.

Around 13,000 people of all ages are diagnosed with a brain tumour every year in the UK alone. Around 5000 of these are cases of primary brain tumours. Furthermore, the incidence of brain tumours has increased by approximately 10 per cent over the decade 1991–2000.

According to Brain Tumour UK, brain tumours are the most common type of solid tumour in children. Childhood cancers are the main cause of death in children, after accidents, with brain tumours accounting for 30 per cent of these deaths.[1] While my son's condition presented challenges unique to cancer and unique to him, my experience of caring for him gave me insight into parenting a child with long-term illness. My experiences may resonate with your experiences. There is much to be gained in learning about each other's approaches to parenting a child with a chronic illness.

As a society, we need to recognize the impact of living with chronic illness. In the case of a brain tumour, the repercussions of surgery, chemotherapy and radiotherapy are far-reaching and, while society acknowledges the obvious difficulties of dealing with cancer, the hidden disabilities like short-term memory loss, chronic fatigue, impaired vision or hearing, diminished self-esteem and self-image issues are often overlooked or not fully appreciated, especially in children.

Many chronic illnesses cause a variety of problems and limitations that have varying degrees of impact on the child and subsequently the whole family. Specific symptoms and problems arise from different conditions, varying in intensity and the need for treatment. All chronic conditions can bring about changes both physically and psychologically. For example, the condition may impede the child intellectually, requiring a change of school. There may be physical problems which necessitate adaptations to the family home to provide easier access and mobility. The treatment required to manage the condition may be arduous and lengthy, requiring one or both of the parents to be with the child in hospital for long periods of time. Also the financial burden of chronic illness will have an impact on the family, the degree depending on their socio-economic position. These changes affect the whole family, and therefore health professionals need to be aware of how integral the child's illness is to the family unit and how it has an impact on all family members.

Brain tumours and other chronic illnesses can strike at random. While it is thought that genetics and environment may be factors in developing a brain tumour, no particular cause has been proven. While chronic illnesses are varied in their effects, symptoms and treatment, there exists a common ground of how we as parents react and cope. However, although we can assert areas of commonality and shared experiences, we must also respect the individual aspect of enduring chronic illness. No two children or families are the same, yet in sharing experiences and information we are better able to cope and tolerate the difficulties.

While Owen endured the overwhelming nausea and tiredness induced by chemotherapy, and was assaulted with repeated blood tests and scans, he managed to retain his sense of 'normality'. He was still a little boy who loved to play and learn. Through his example we learned as a family that the greatest gift we could give Owen was to be normal. While we were devastated by Owen's diagnosis, we decided early on that we would do everything in our power to help him enjoy life. This included being upbeat and happy when we often felt the reverse. We believed that he shouldn't carry the burden of our grief. While we recognized that the 25 per cent chance of his survival was slim, we lived with acceptance of this prognosis. This was not surrender. To be realistic about the prognosis enabled a greater strength. We were better able to research the condition and to question doctors when we understood the probable outcomes.

Our aim was to enable Owen to live the fullest life possible under the constraints of regular hospital stays and an impaired immune system due to chemotherapy.

Chronic illness became a part of our lives that limited us in many ways, but we learned to live with the difficulties while not allowing them to encroach on Owen's quality of life as far as we possibly could.

Foreword

This book by Sharon Dempsey is a valuable addition to the literature on chronic paediatric illness. It provides a very clear picture of the parents' perspective of the journey forced on families by chronic illness. It is primarily intended for parents, and those who read it will gain a great deal of information to help them make the most of the situation for their children, their families and themselves. Nevertheless, it also has considerable value for all practitioners, whether they have a major role in this area (e.g. paediatricians and nurses) or simply come across children with long-term illness in the course of their usual practice (e.g. teachers).

It is written with sincerity and clarity derived from Sharon's own experiences with her son, Owen, who was ill for some years and eventually died at home. She gained a great deal from this experience and has found the strength to share it with others in this book. Parenting is challenging in any circumstances, but the difficulties multiply enormously in the context of chronic illness, since the care of the child is more dependent upon parents than anyone else; the stakes are high and the journey is tough.

The book provides an in-depth understanding of the path through chronic illness, illustrating the obvious effects on the child, but also on the parents, siblings and the family as a whole across the spectrum, from the psychological and social to the physical. It begins with the onset of the illness and disclosure of the diagnosis and finishes with the circumstances where a child is dying. It is highlighted throughout with specific examples from Sharon's own experience with Owen. She clearly presents the many challenges faced at all stages and the need for holistic support from multiple sources, including the medical/surgical team, other agencies, extended family, friends, the community more generally and voluntary services.

Sharon offers a balanced view of the situation, acknowledging the difficulties as well as the joys, the similarities but also the extreme variability of conditions and the uniqueness of each family's response to disease. She sees the problem holistically from a family-centred and strengths-based perspective, considering all aspects of care in the community, including schooling. Relationships and communication have a central place throughout the book and there is a strong and explicit notion of partnership between parents and healthcare providers. Although this is never easy to achieve and demands a great deal of parents and the healthcare team, the benefits for the quality of life of the child and family are worth the effort.

There is much to be learnt from this book and it deserves careful reading.

Hilton Davis
Emeritus Professor of Child Health
Psychology, King's College London

Introduction

Extreme Parenting: Parenting Your Child with a Chronic Illness is an exploration of parenting under extreme circumstances. Parents are the primary focus of this book, but I have also written this book to provide insights for the range of professionals who help to support families where a child has a chronic illness. In helping parents to cope with their child's condition, we are assisting the child. When a child is diagnosed with a serious illness or condition, the ability of the parent to cope is of paramount importance to the welfare of the child. Medics can provide treatment protocols, but the success of treatment can often depend on how the parents, as the primary care givers, implement care for the child. It is estimated that more than one-tenth of children suffer from chronic illness, with vast differences between the severity and impact of the symptoms.

Advances in science and medical interventions have seen more children and young people than ever living with chronic illnesses that previously would have resulted in early death. This has led to an increase in the responsibility placed on families to administer care at sophisticated levels. For some families, intense care giving begins with the birth of the child, while others experience normality before the onset of disease, the advent of infection or the manifestation of a condition.

How families cope depends on the severity and nature of the condition, and how they are affected by it. Many children live with conditions like asthma, epilepsy or eczema with relatively little impact on their lives except for flare-up periods. Some conditions can be managed easily although they present problems with the need for the child to comply with treatment and manage their condition successfully, such as in the case of diabetes. There are other extremes, such as cystic fibrosis, some cancers, sickle cell anaemia or chronic kidney disease, which have long-term implications and progressively worsen, leaving some children in chronic pain and severely disabled.

A chronic illness or condition is defined by the US National Center for Health Statistics as being a serious health problem that lasts beyond three months, usually causes disability, disfigurement or physical limitations and involves special diets, medical interventions and the need for follow-up treatment and ongoing care in the home environment.

Chronic illnesses are treatable or manageable but usually not curable. There may be periods of acute illness and crisis periods. Illnesses such as some cancers, diabetes, epilepsy, HIV/AIDS, cystic fibrosis, juvenile arthritis, eczema, certain heart conditions and asthma are just some of the diseases that come under the remit of chronic illness. While these conditions can affect a child physically in vastly different ways, they have much in common with regards to the psychological wellbeing of the child. Some conditions can be controlled by medication and others can be in remission for a period of time.

We all evolve as parents. As our children grow and develop, so do we. Parenting strategies employed when dealing with a toddler will differ from those we use when dealing with an adolescent. This is also true for parenting the child with a chronic illness. We cannot assume that one strategy, or one set of suggestions, will work for every child, at every stage of their development. The child with a chronic illness will grow and develop, and each stage will bring with it a new set of challenges.

The role of parents as active participants in children's healthcare in becoming treatment providers and carers has changed the relationship between families and doctors. Long gone are the days when children were deposited on hospital wards to be visited by their parents at set times in the day. Doctors are no longer revered and unchallenged.

For the role of parent as healthcare provider to be successful, the parents must be knowledgeable about their child's condition. Parents are the experts on their child and they become the experts on their child's condition. Doctors depend on parents to help them achieve the best possible care for the child. In working together, parents and doctors are able to deliver the best healthcare possible. Treating and caring for children with chronic illness has become a collaborative undertaking with parents and doctors working in partnership.

Ultimately the illness affects the entire family. It is a whole family experience and how the ill child copes is dependent on how the entire family is supported.

I intend this book to be a source of support for families embarking on the journey of parenting in difficult circumstances. Every child is different and, while there are common factors in the effects of all chronic illnesses on families, I cannot emphasize enough that you know your child better than anyone. You have their interests and welfare at heart and, while I can advise and relate to your situation, I cannot make decisions for your child. There is no one solution or easy remedy. We all struggle from time to time, but we can all cope in the most difficult of circumstances. *I can tell you that you are not alone in caring for your ill child.* Advances in healthcare and medicine have resulted in more children surviving conditions that previously would have resulted in premature death.

The prognosis of a child living with a chronic condition can be, in part, dependent on the coping ability of their family. A family that copes is more likely to follow treatment and care plans, and be active in seeking support. It is therefore in the interests of the health professionals to ensure that the family is given the utmost support in caring for their child.

Families caring for a child with a chronic illness can benefit from strategies that enable them to relieve stress, share their responsibilities, gain support and explore their emotional anxieties. For some people, an effective strategy is one that provides them with time out; space to think and process their emotions away from the pressures of home and hospital. Another parent may need to maintain constant contact with their ill child but appreciate support with their other children. Others find empowerment through becoming knowledgeable about the condition, and gain a sense of control in understanding the illness. Some seek out support groups and find strength in sharing their anxieties. For some, religion offers the greatest solace and strength.

We are all different and meet the challenges of parenting in different ways. The parent who recognizes a successful strategy and employs it to good advantage will cope better and be a more effective parent.

In recognizing the benefits of seeking out information that offers strategies to manage a child's illness and the effects of living with a chronic condition, families are empowered. Through gaining a sense of empowerment, parents feel more confident and their self-esteem is enhanced. They *feel* better able to cope and this in turn becomes reality – they *do* cope.

Sadly, in some instances, the family can disintegrate under the pressure of caring for a child with a chronic illness. This does not have to be the expected outcome. In most cases, the experience of loving and caring for a child with a chronic illness can be a positive, life-affirming one. While no one would wish for their child to be ill, let alone suffer from a debilitating, sometimes life-threatening condition, we can find our relationships and family life to be enriched by the experience.

This book can offer advice and reassurance, but it is never going to represent the experiences of every parent with a child who is chronically ill – this book draws on my own experiences, but I have attempted to consider the needs of all parents wherever possible. From the moment of diagnosis, the family has to adapt to a new reality. The dynamics of family life are altered. Eventually, a new order emerges and the family begins the journey of coping with chronic illness. Care plans, treatment and support must be organized, and this book suggests ways to make these run as smoothly as possible. I will cover education and issues surrounding schooling and the need to feel included in the community. Central to this book is the need to communicate effectively with your child, with the medics and with the wider family and support network. Communication will form part of every chapter and, by developing strategies to assist you in communicating, you will be in a stronger position to deal with the demands placed upon you.

This book will also examine how health professionals and those working with children that have a chronic illness can better address the needs of the whole family. Identification of what will cause stress, and anticipation of crisis periods, will help prepare the family and aid them in coping. Through understanding how chronic illness has an impact on the parents and siblings as well as the child, professionals can devise strategies to incorporate the whole family in the care management process and, in doing so, help the child with a chronic illness both in psychosocial and physical terms.

The Diagnosis Disclosure

The term 'chronic illness' is used to describe an array of conditions which cause long-term health problems or disability. Characteristics of chronic illness typically include a progressive condition or disease, which often cannot be cured but can at best be managed. Chronic illness can be acquired as in a brain injury, it can be the lasting result of infection as in meningitis, or it can be a genetic disorder. Diseases such as asthma and eczema are the most common chronic illnesses in children. While some childhood cancers can be cured, they are chronic conditions in that they require long-term treatment and have a lasting effect on the wellbeing of the child.

While symptoms vary between illnesses, we can identify common factors in how parents react to diagnoses. There are also identifiable strategies for coping with the challenges that arise through parenting a child with a chronic illness.

Chronic illness is usually for life. It can be a slow developing condition or one that has been undiagnosed for a long period of time. The term is used to describe a variety of illnesses from cancer to diabetes, to spina bifida, acquired immunodeficiency, congenital heart diseases, cystic fibrosis or an acquired brain injury. These conditions are rare but, when we consider them together as chronic illnesses, many children and young people are affected. In turn, when we consider the effect on the family as a unit, the number of people affected by chronic illness whether directly or indirectly is substantial.

While it is unlikely that a chronic illness will ever be cured, a period of chronic illness absence is referred to as remission. The child can experience periods of being well, of living without treatment or symptoms, but the threat of recurrence is constant. This unpredictability in itself causes anxiety and stress. It is believed that between 10 and 20 per cent of children endure long-term illness or health problems. These health problems have a dual impact on the physical and psychological welfare of the child.

The child affected by chronic illness can be obviously disabled by their condition or it can be an 'invisible' disability as in the case of asthma. The physical disabilities require ongoing medical intervention and occupational support. Learning difficulties can demand a change of school and have an impact on the child's social interaction. For instance, a child who has experienced a head injury or brain infection may no longer have the same ability to concentrate or retain information. They may find that their needs are better met at a different school. Certain conditions like cystic fibrosis demand daily intensive physiotherapy; eczema requires regular applications of ointments, bathing in a special bath solution and even bandaging before sleep. Acute lymphoblastic leukaemia (ALL) is another demanding condition. Boys tend to have a higher relapse rate than girls and can require up to three years of chemotherapy treatment, with girls being treated for two years. The range of the different demands placed on the child and the family seems endless. Underlying the differences is the fact that they all have an impact on the psychological and social functioning of the child and the family.

All parents set out with expectations, hopes and dreams for their child. When a child is diagnosed with a health problem, these aspirations are altered. While one parent is hoping to see their child graduate from university, another is praying that they can live pain free. A definitive diagnosis of a health problem can be a relief when a family has lived with uncertainty and unexplained symptoms for some time. When a diagnosis has come following months or even years of attending hospitals and seeking medical advice, it can mark the end of a period of seemingly battling with health professionals.

Coping with the diagnosis

Diagnosis of a chronic condition is devastating and can often induce a state of grief.[1] A parent can experience grief for the life they had planned or imagined for their child. There is a sense of loss on many levels: loss of control, loss of the old life, loss of time with the child, and loss of the life that the parent thought they had created for themselves and their family. In recognizing the onset of a grieving period following the diagnosis, the parent is better prepared in coping with the emotions of shock, denial and even anger.

In some instances, the diagnosis can be unexpected and come as a shock. It is natural for a parent to question why an illness has struck their child. They may feel isolated and angry. Some parents enter a period of denial – a significant stage in the grieving process. Newly bereaved people often speak of their disbelief, their inability to accept the death of a loved one. They are often in shock. For the parent of a newly diagnosed child, denial is almost natural. They don't *want* to believe what they are being told and seek second opinions hoping to prove the medics wrong. The mother of a child diagnosed with Hurler's syndrome, also known as mucopolysaccharidosis type I (MPS I), described her feelings following the diagnosis disclosure:

> My initial reaction was that I wanted the doctor to keep my child and I wanted to run away. I just could not face the fact that I would lose him. Whenever I got home I put him to bed and tried to distance myself from him – I was filled with horror. However, whenever he cried to be lifted I went upstairs and whenever I opened his door he smiled to see me. At this my heart just melted and I promised him that every day I had with him would be a good day – no tears – I was determined to enjoy every last minute with him and I certainly did.

Denial is part of the adjustment process. It is as if the conscious mind cannot yet accept the new reality and enters into a period of denial to allow for change and adaptation. Denial can take on the form of optimism, hoping and asserting that the prognosis is wrong and that a cure will materialize. When one parent enters into this form of denial, they can alienate the other parent and this can cause conflict. While one parent is struggling to adapt to the diagnosis, the other is experiencing disbelief and can be dismissive of concerns. Denial is in many ways a defence mechanism, unconsciously employed, and normally does not last long. Open communication with the medics, as well as time, enables realism to creep in.

Difficulties can arise when one parent is experiencing a different stage of the emotional array than the other. It is important to try to work together, to accommodate each other's highs and lows. If one parent is feeling overwhelmed and negative about the future, the other parent can present a more balanced, reasonable assessment. At times, it can feel as if both parents are at odds with each other, without ever reaching a position of common understanding. This is normal: no two people will react in the same way to any given situation and, in recognizing this, they can each be more forgiving and accommodating.

Anger and frustration are common emotions at the time of diagnosis. Why me? Why my child? The obvious answer to this question is, *why not?* There are no equations for life to work out perfectly or justly. Nobody can insure against bad health. All parents feel a sense of guilt – are their children eating a balanced diet, are they reading the right books, watching too much television, doing well at school? When a parent is faced with a diagnosis of chronic illness, they often assume they are in some way responsible. Guilt, like anger, is a negative, wasteful emotion. The parent of a child with a chronic illness cannot afford to indulge in guilt – it is a drain on their emotional wellbeing and achieves nothing. The diagnosis of inherited diseases can lead to parents feeling intense guilt and responsibility for their child's condition. They can then enter into a blame scenario, causing unnecessary anger and pain for each other.

For some parents, guilt is a huge burden. The cause of most chronic illnesses is unclear, but we often assume responsibility. Even if the condition is inherited, it is illogical and wasteful to attribute blame. You need all your emotional reserves to deal with your child. If it is at all possible, rationalize with yourself that you cannot be blamed for your child's illness.

Unfortunately, in life random illnesses and injuries strike. Often we have no way of knowing why. Chronic illness can occur following infection, genetic defects or the result of an injury. Many cancers can be life threatening and affect a child for the many years during which treatment is given. We cannot control our child's health trajectory.

The period of adaptation and acceptance varies. If a medical problem has gone undiagnosed for a long period of time, the diagnosis and the possibility of dealing with the problems and symptoms can be welcomed and the family is better able to accept the diagnosis and begin the process of adapting.

It is easy to feel isolated from so-called normal society. A chronic illness, which renders a child disabled or extremely sick, sets the family apart. Friends and family can sympathize and offer support, but they can never really know the extent of the emotional and physical demands. Alienation and isolation are common factors. You feel alone. The enormity of what lies ahead cannot be under-estimated, but how can you adequately explain your deepest fears? In not being able to communicate your worries, you feel alienated from those closest to you. One parent described herself as having a new identity: 'I was the mother of the sick child.' She saw herself as being labelled.

Most family and friends will try to offer positive thoughts. Contrary to what you are thinking, they will tell you not to worry, that doctors often give the worst possible scenario, that medical science is making advances all the time. You will want to scream. Those around you will want to hope for the best possible outcome, sometimes at the expense of all reason. This can be frustrating. Coming to terms with the diagnosis is difficult enought without the sense of defeatism you feel about the attitude of friends and family. Accepting the reality of the diagnosis is a more positive approach. Acceptance does not exclude hope.

While you are contemplating the impact of the illness on your child in the present, your mind will inevitably leap ahead to the future. Will they manage to have a fulfilling life or an independent life? Will girlfriends or boyfriends be beyond their expectations? These questions and many others linked to the unknown future will haunt you if you let them. Focus on the immediate. Dealing with the here and now is enough.

Positive thinking and upbeat attitudes can be a source of irritation and also be demoralizing. You are made to feel as if you have given up too easily if you don't believe that there is a magical cure around the corner. Try not to waste energy or emotion living with false hope. While being wary of hoping against all reason, it is also necessary to avoid despair. Trying to find somewhere between the extremes of hope and despair is difficult and at times you will fluctuate from one end of the spectrum to the other. Having an awareness of how false hope can be damaging is half the battle. To hide behind false hope is to avoid dealing with the problems in hand. Despair is also a means of escape. To despair is to give up and a sick child needs all your uncompromised support. Despair can be a self-indulgent emotion like guilt. It is all about the individual feeling the despair, not the child who needs untarnished energies.

To accept a devastating prognosis is not to give up on your child; instead, it is the first step in exceptional parenting – to accept the realities as presented in order to do your utmost for your child. Decisions should be made with realistic probabilities in mind. This is not to say that this is living without hope. On the contrary, real hope will carry you through the darkest moments.

Most parents feel overwhelmed by a sense of powerlessness. When a child is diagnosed with a chronic condition, we lose our sense of control. Some parents experience periods of helplessness and inadequacy. It is difficult to absorb information when you are in a state of shock. Many parents want to shut down and not be told much about the condition, in order to protect themselves from the devastation.

Doctors can offer a diagnosis, treatment protocols and management of the condition. In some instances though, they can only offer monitoring. When a diagnosis is terminal, treatment is palliative. Living with the knowledge that a child is terminally ill is a huge strain. The long goodbye is often the most difficult.

The child's best advocate is its parents. How the parent copes with the diagnosis affects how the child copes. While it feels impossible to deal with the uncertainty ahead, it is important for the child's wellbeing that those closest to them are positive and upbeat. It is easy to let the diagnosis make you a victim or a hostage to the condition. Remember it is a huge part of your child's life but not the whole of your child. Illness affects the child but does not define them. They were your child before the diagnosis and they are still your child.

The role of the parent as advocate can be a huge pressure and responsibility. There exists a dichotomy between advocating, working in partnership with the medics and sometimes being in conflict with them. Some parents feel that the two roles are conflictual: that in caring for the child the parent is all consumed, and that it is not their job but the job of the medics to control treatment and care plans.

Sometimes parents feel that in raising concerns over treatment and questioning doctors they are subjecting their child to unfair treatment; or that the doctor will resent the parent's attitude and feel less inclined to be actively involved with the child. Doctors are trained to work with parents. They realize it is in their best interests to listen to parents and to take their opinions seriously. When difficulties arise, the medics should be professional and not feel biased against the child. After all, the parent is experiencing a time of great stress, and they are worried and anxious about their child. If relations with the medic are strained, the medic should be able to understand the source of the parent's concerns and set about answering their questions to their satisfaction. An anxious parent may appear aggressive, but their anger is most likely born out of frustration and fear.

Good practice dictates that, when a diagnosis of chronic illness is being delivered, the doctor has other staff members present to support the parents. This can be nursing staff and sometimes hospital social workers. It is often the nursing staff or the hospital social worker who the parents turn to with questions when they begin to absorb the information they have been given. Nursing staff seem more approachable and are more likely to explain a condition in easy-to-understand terms.

No two diagnosis encounters are the same. While we can hope that good practice and communication training will dictate that the diagnosis is imparted in sympathetic and supportive terms, not all parents are so fortunate. Not so long ago it was common for doctors giving damning diagnoses to advise parents to place their child in care and to move on and have another. Thankfully now, we can expect a more understanding and sympathetic approach. Health professionals need to recognize the value of parents as part of the care team. They must work in conjunction with parents to provide a way forward from the point of diagnosis. In order to make informed choices, parents need to be part of a shared decision-making process.

How a diagnosis is handled can have a significant and lasting effect on how parents cope.[2]

I can clearly remember the consultant telling my husband and me that our son had a mass of tumour in the back of his head, and trying to control his own tears as he witnessed our devastation. I shall always be grateful that this consultant, whom we had only met a couple of hours previously, treated us, and, more importantly, Owen, with such compassion. It was easier to trust him knowing that he cared about our son and us.

Many parents speak of the trauma and subsequent anger at the way in which they were told of their child's condition. If a diagnosis is not handled well, it can irreparably damage the parent/doctor relationship. Doctors need to take into account how a diagnosis of a chronic condition can affect the parents. They can feel shock and disbelief, or even anger, which can be misplaced and directed towards the medical profession. When a parent is faced with a poor prognosis, they are distraught. If the medical profession explains the diagnosis in a sympathetic, caring fashion, then they will be helping to form a more positive, supportive relationship with the family from the beginning. There is a vast difference between doctors in how they convey devastating news to parents. As one parent described, the difference from one medic to the next is dependent on their skill and compassion. It has been asserted that families who require intervention later on in a child's illness can be identified by how they coped during the diagnosis period. The impact of the diagnosis, and how it is handled by the doctor disclosing the information and the parent receiving it, can have a lasting impression.

Dr Anthony McCarthy, Owen's first paediatric oncologist, believes that there a number of ways for the medical profession to help parents at the time of diagnosis. He recognizes that the shock of the diagnosis means that parents find it difficult to absorb information at the time of initial disclosure:

> I think it is important to try and limit their first meeting to passing on the diagnosis and a broad outline of the management without going into any great details. We are well aware that most parents hear very little after the word 'cancer' has been spoken. A second meeting would be arranged for the following day so that further information can be then passed on.
>
> I would always advise parents to take out a paper and pen and have it by their bed so that they can write down questions which tend to hit them in the middle of the night. When arranging any such meeting we try to arrange a place that is quiet and free from any disruption. It is always preferable to have both parents present at this meeting and if that were not possible either a grandparent or a

good friend. From the medical point of view we always tend to have a nurse or social worker present. These extra people are there to try and help the parent take in and understand the information they have been given.

Often the diagnosis means very little to the parents because they have yet to discover how the condition will affect their child. If the disease is familiar to the parents, there is still the uncertainty of the impact it will have. The process of learning about the illness begins with the diagnosis. The parents will acquire knowledge about symptoms, statistical outcomes, treatment, drugs, further testing: it is all overwhelming. One carer who worked with children diagnosed with cancer said, 'I would hope that the doctors realize that the parents are hearing the diagnosis for the first time, even though they are repeating it for the hundredth.'

When this person's own son was diagnosed with cerebral palsy, she found that the doctor presented the worst case scenario. As she described it, 'They were quite brutal in what they said.'

The family undergoes a transition period in which they all learn to adapt to their new reality. The parent becomes a parent/care giver. Parents adjust at differing rates. Some accept the diagnosis more readily because they have suspected a problem, while others are shocked. One couple found that they needed different periods of time to face the diagnosis. As the mother described their experience, she said:

> My husband unfortunately did not feel there was anything wrong with the child so the shock of his diagnosis had a profound effect on him. He hardly communicated for six months and the weight fell off him.

> I had three other children plus my ill child to cope with and I could not take his feelings on board. I just gave him the time he needed to face up to the problems. After this he was able to cope much better and gave me lots of help with the child. The child would only allow him to put him to bed and every night he knew exactly the time he would return from work and he waited in the hall for him.

The child with a chronic illness also experiences this period of transition and, unless they are fully involved in communication with parents and health professionals, they will feel isolated and alone. It is a relatively recent phenomenon to communicate with children about their medical conditions. Children were considered to be better off not knowing what was wrong with them. This lack of inclusion and involvement, rather than being an act of protection, denies the child the opportunity to process the information and adapt accordingly.

Despite the trauma of the diagnosis period, parents can identify and acknowledge when a diagnosis disclosure is handled well. One mother felt that she could trust the consultant to explain the diagnosis of a brain tumour to her four-year-old son following his sensitive and gentle handling of the diagnosis disclosure to her. She instinctively felt that the surgeon could explain the diagnosis to the child in age-appropriate terms better than she could: 'We didn't have time to think of how to put this into a four-year-old's language. What he said gave us a good basis of how to go forward and talk to Daniel later.'

The child will have a better chance of coping and ultimately co-operating and responding to treatment if they have an understanding of the illness. Even the youngest of children can be educated about their illness, in age and developmentally appropriate terms. Knowledge eliminates fear.

The diagnosis time has been identified as a critical period for families.[3] Parents, too, will speak of the diagnosis as being the worst time. Hospitals should have a private room where parents can be told. They need information in straightforward language, and time to absorb it. They should be given time alone after the diagnosis has been explained, and offered the opportunity to ask questions at a later time when they have absorbed the information. While families need information and education about their child's condition, they also need emotional support from their medics. Doctors must develop a sense of empathy, to be able to relate to the parents' anguish and to appreciate that the news they are imparting to the family is of grave significance.[4]

Parents often experience a sense of guilt and blame at the diagnosis. One mother said:

> I felt as if I'd done something wrong. I blamed myself. My self-confidence as a mother was damaged for ever.

> I felt very alone. So much was going on and I was on my own. It was as if I was in a glass box and I couldn't reach out or do anything about it. It was a complete loss of control.

It can be difficult for a parent to listen to the information being given when instinctively they do not want to hear bad news. Your every instinct is to say 'no' and shut out what you are being told – to refuse to accept what you are being told in a vain effort to prevent it from being real. One mother said she felt disbelief because her daughter seemed well: 'I thought, "Is this really happening?" It just didn't go in. It took a while for the illness to manifest itself and because she appeared normal I thought there was a chance they were mistaken.'

It is useful for a parent to have an informal advocate to sit in on the parent/doctor conference. This can be a friend, relative, nurse or hospital social worker. An advocate can help when the parent is finding it difficult to absorb the information. It is useful for parents or their advocate to be given a pen and paper to take notes. Medical terminology and jargon needs to be explained in straightforward, accessible language. For instance, following Owen's CT scan, we could have been told that he had tumours in the neuroepithelial lining of the fourth ventricle. Instead we were told that the scan had shown a mass at the back of his head. A mass of tumour in the back of his head sounds blunt but that is what it is. No amount of jargon could have softened the impact of the diagnosis. Medical terminology can alienate parents. They can feel inadequate because they do not understand the terminology. However, medics must also avoid patronizing parents by making assumptions about their level of understanding. Dr McCarthy tries to clarify exactly what the parents understand about the condition at the outset:

> I find it important to ask parents from the very beginning what exactly they know and understand of their child's condition before disclosing any information of results of tests. By doing this one 'clears the playing field' and this does help to try and prevent any misinformation or misunderstanding taking place.

It is not unreasonable to challenge a diagnosis and to want a second opinion. Seeking a second opinion can provide confirmation of the diagnosis and offer a different perspective of the prognosis. Doctors are not infallible and a second opinion is insurance against a wrong diagnosis. A second opinion also provides a wider remit for consultation on prognosis and treatment plans. Shared information and research between hospitals and countries is commonplace, but sometimes doctors and hospitals have differing approaches and it is worth investigating alternative treatments.

Parents should not be afraid to voice fears and concerns. Never feel that your question is too trivial – ask yourself, 'Is this important to my child?' Remember you are the expert on your child, but the doctor is the expert on the illness. At the point of diagnosis you embark on a steep learning curve and it is not unreasonable to expect clinicians to be supportive in that learning process. The medics must also learn about the child and its family.

Doctors sometimes advise against trawling the internet for information for fear that parents are misled or interpret information wrongly, but ultimately information is valuable. Sometimes you have to know a little in order to know which questions to ask. Researching the condition can also provide a sense of control and empowerment – you are doing something active to help your child. However, it is necessary for parents to be guided by doctors because parents need to have a clear understanding of the information and how it pertains to their child's individual health condition.

Families should work with the medical team and ask them which websites are recommended and which journals to read. At the outset of the diagnosis, it is important to gain an understanding of the condition and the prognosis through research. Parents can become experts on their child's condition through use of the internet. From our homes we can read realms of research and compare treatment and healthcare policies throughout the world. Before the advent of the internet, researching medical conditions was time-consuming and difficult, but now firing keywords into a search engine delivers information to us in an instant.

Physiotherapist Finola Beattie, who works with children living with cerebral palsy and cystic fibrosis, has found that parents need information to help them cope. For some parents, taking control of their child's condition and researching it thoroughly is a coping strategy in itself:

> Parents are no longer intimidated to ask questions. They have researched their child's condition on the internet and know a hundred times more than we do. It has changed so much because they can get the information readily. They become the expert on their child's condition.

> Some parents find that this is a way of coping. By taking control they can remain positive because they know what the next step will be. Different things work for different people but it does amaze me how parents do cope and just get on with it.

Forget the statistics – they can be demoralizing. No one has certainties in life. It is easy to waste energy and emotion on weighing up the odds. Sometimes it is necessary to be aware of statistical outcomes when making informed decisions about treatment but, on the whole, statistics are merely guides. It is usually at the point of diagnosis that statistics seem most important. Doctors often use statistics to put the illness in some sort of context. Statistics are nothing more than odds – an indication at best.

Following the diagnosis, it is tempting to turn to those who offer an over-optimistic assessment. It would help if parents learned to differentiate between realism and conjecture. Hope can be sustaining and help parents to cope, but they should be wary of false hope. It can be too easy to fall prey to unscrupulous people offering remedies or cures. Even within the mainstream medical profession, there are medics who are willing to take risks with pioneering techniques or treatments. At the time of Owen's diagnosis, a documentary showed a prominent American neurosurgeon who was successful in operating on children with previously considered inoperable brain tumours. Desperate to know if we should approach him, we did some research and spoke to our neurosurgeon, who smiled knowingly before explaining, yes, this surgeon would be aggressive and remove all the tumour but, in doing so, he would also remove a substantial part of Owen's brain. Be mindful of anyone promising a cure when the doctors who have treated your child have advised that a cure is not viable. However, that is not to say that investigation is pointless. Medical science is developing and new techniques do emerge.

Facing an uncertain future is one of the worst aspects of dealing with chronic illness. At the time of diagnosis, doctors can advise parents on probable outcomes, but often it is a process of discovery for the medics and parents alike. Chronic illnesses can present a variety of symptoms that vary in their intensity and impact. Sometimes life can seem manageable and good, and at other times crisis strikes. Chronic illness is subject to change and variation. The disease or condition can progress and worsen or the child can enter a period of remission. Normal developmental changes and growth can also have an impact on the condition. Parents experience a kaleidoscope of emotions; while they are coming to terms with one aspect of the condition, something else can materialize necessitating a new routine of care management. The fluidity of the situation is in itself a cause of stress. There is a constant need for adaptability.

Telling your child

Fear of the unknown is a huge issue for a child. A child with chronic illness lives a life of uncertainty. They fear the unpredictable problems that can arise, and may feel insecure and alienated from their apparently carefree peers. Even the youngest of children need to be reassured. Children and particularly adolescents resent feeling different from their peers. They want to fit in, and chronic illness can be an obstacle to being perceived as normal. Just as parents find the time of diagnosis traumatic, so too can the child. Children's reactions to diagnosis often mirror those of their parents, and are dependent on their age and developmental understanding. Their need for information about the illness and their understanding of its impact on them will develop as they grow.

Many children will be in hospital at the time of diagnosis, following tests and explorations. Hospitals can be intimidating and frightening places for a child. Most hospitals try to be comfortable and welcoming for children, but the need for tests and procedures can cause fear and uncertainty. It is crucial not to overwhelm the child with too much information. Answer their questions as truthfully as possible; if a procedure is going to hurt and a parent lies, the child will learn that they cannot trust them or the medics. It helps if the child can understand that the medics are helping, in that they are working to make them well, or as well as can be. The parent is the best judge of how much information the child should be given. It is best to speak about the immediate present, and to discuss hospital stays, treatment plans and the nature of the illness in age-appropriate terms.

There are many books published that deal with hospital treatment, and some publishers produce books relating to specific conditions. A young child can look at picture books about hospitals to provide them with a reference with which to compare their own experiences. This enables the parent to talk about the doctors and nurses in a positive way, and to open up a conversation that allows the child to ask questions.

Parents should seek out the hospital play therapist. They are trained to help children cope with medical procedures, and are useful in helping to communicate illness to young children. Many hospital therapists have dolls fitted with intravenous lines to enable the child to practise taking blood from them. Practising physiotherapy on a doll can help a young child with cystic fibrosis understand the need for them to have regular physiotherapy. Working with dolls in play situations enables the child to have some control over their situation. They can play out various scenarios that have worried them, and work through their concerns in an environment in which they feel safe and secure.

Some children avoid discussing their illness with their parents for fear of upsetting them. If they have witnessed a parent's distress, they may feel responsible and guilty for being ill. This can be a terrible burden. However, it is not always wrong for a child to see how much their parent is affected by the diagnosis. This can reinforce the idea that the parent is involved and will be with the child every step of the way. They are not experiencing their illness alone.

Communication at the time of diagnosis is vital. Allow the child to talk about their concerns and worries. They may have questions that they want to ask the medics, and they should be given the opportunity to do this alone if they so desire. The age of the child will dictate the level of information given, but I have found that even from the age of two a child is able to take on board some of the medical terminology and to learn something about their illness and its impact. Just as parents can gain a greater sense of control through learning more about the illness, so too can the child.

Parents who choose not to inform the child about their specific illness, preferring instead to talk in vague terms about viruses or infections, are misguided and may even put the child at risk. The child who understands their condition is able to develop an awareness of their limitations and to work within them. They are also more able to cope with the pressures of explaining their condition to their peers. The child left with no clear information has only anxiety and worry. They know they are ill, they have experience of symptoms and have been subjected to medical investigations, they have heard the doctors and family speak of their condition, yet it is so serious that they cannot be told of its true nature. This can lead them to assume only the worst when often that does not have to be the reality.

Knowledge gives the child 'ownership' of their condition. They can foster a better relationship with their medics if they have some sort of understanding about why they need to have treatment, or why they face limitations in what they can do. Ownership of their condition also enables a greater sense of responsibility, which can be necessary when the child needs to be entrusted to explain their condition in situations when they are without their parents. For instance, it is crucial for a child with a peanut allergy to learn to make responsible decisions when eating outside the family home. They must be knowledgeable about their condition and informed about safe foods and unsafe foods. It is also important for a child with a peanut allergy to carry adrenaline in the form of an 'Epipen'. They need to 'own' the information of how to use it and to be responsible enough to ensure it is with them at all times. Likewise, a child with diabetes must be responsible for their diet and compliant in their treatment. This is not to burden the child with responsibility. The age and developmental stage of the child is relevant to the degree of responsibility that they can assume.

A diagnosis of chronic illness can raise questions about a person's identity. It is easy to become the 'patient', to be a victim of the illness or condition. The parent can question their role too. They seek to re-establish their relationship with the child as a primary medical care giver as well as parent. The readjustments are part of the process of accepting the new normality in the family dynamic. Parents can feel particularly vulnerable when a child is diagnosed. The life they thought they had designed is suddenly altered and they enter a period of great uncertainty. Plans for the future are dismantled and it seems impossible to know what the next day will bring. This lack of control over the future can cause a sense of hopelessness and helplessness. In becoming better informed about the condition and its treatment, the parent can assume a new sense of control and coping ability.

The impact on the family

Communication with siblings at the time of diagnosis is of paramount importance (see Chapter 3, Communication: A Two-way Street). Chronic illness does not affect only the sick child. Siblings can feel frightened and lonely when they experience chronic illness in the family. It is easy to overlook the needs of the well children when dealing with hospital stays, etc. At the time of diagnosis, the ill sibling and parents can suddenly be taken away from home to spend time at the hospital, perhaps even without explanation. This sudden absence can be damaging even if the siblings are being cared for by close relatives. One mother found that she became so involved with her sick child that the well siblings were often overlooked:

> I spent at least two days per week going to different appointments and clinics with him. This meant my other children came home to an empty house, something which would never have happened. My child became the focal point in my life – he needed me more so therefore I gave him everything.

It is understandable that the parent may not want to explain too much to the siblings until they have a fuller understanding of the diagnosis themselves, but it is necessary to enable the siblings to be part of the process of *discovering* the illness. As the symptoms unfold and the diagnosis becomes clear, it is sometimes a gradual process. If the siblings have an awareness of this process, then the diagnosis will be less surprising. Explain that the child is sick, discuss the previous health problems if there have been some and ask the siblings' opinions on how they feel they can help. Inclusion in the process will aid the siblings' acceptance of the situation and of any changes to day-to-day arrangements.

If a sibling understands the nature of the illness and the impact on their brother or sister, they will want to help. Their understanding of the condition is their 'ownership' – their key to feeling included and more likely to be accommodating to the ill child. Enabling them to assist with play time, physiotherapy or medicine times is a positive way of including them. Siblings can feel jealous or resentful of the apparent extra attention the sick child is receiving. Combat this by giving the sibling ownership of the situation by allowing them to be active participants in the ill child's condition. The whole family is affected, and the whole family should be appreciated and acknowledged as care givers. If possible, organize special treats for all the children. Also, parents should try to spend individual time with the well sibling. Encourage hospital visits or, if this is not possible, help the siblings to make cards or write letters. Ensure that those looking after them during critical times are aware of their fears and concerns. The siblings' schools should also be informed because problems may arise and the teachers will then be better able to put the incident in perspective and offer support. Those caring for the sibling during periods of parental absence need to appreciate that they too have a period of adjustment and acceptance to undergo following the diagnosis.

Learning to live with the diagnosis is the first step in a long process. For some, acceptance is easier because the diagnosis has come following a long period of uncertainty. The diagnosis can be seen in a positive light in that it offers a framework for action. In a small number of cases, a definitive diagnosis is not obtained. Sometimes there are no satisfactory answers. This is difficult and raises many problems, not least a greater sense of uncertainty about what the future might hold. It can be more difficult to access support networks if a known condition cannot be attributed to a child's symptoms. Some conditions have vague, slowly developing symptoms, which do not fit a precise category of disease or condition. There is difficulty for the parents and the child living with a condition that cannot be diagnosed. Support networks are usually centred on particular illnesses. Life with a chronic illness is isolating but, when the condition cannot be attributed to a known illness, there is even less support and sense of belonging.

It is useful to inform other family members and friends about the diagnosis. By talking, the parent can work through their feelings. It is useful to explain that the demands placed on the family will be great, and that the family will welcome assistance with household chores, driving siblings to school, etc. Allowing family and friends to help is vital. Many parents try to cope at the time of diagnosis without help from outside the immediate family unit. Chronic illness is a long haul. Invite family and friends to experience the highs and lows with you. Some people may not always have a positive effect on your morale, but you learn quickly whom to turn to and whom to avoid. Be aware that there will be crisis points when you will need extra help. Explain to your support network that you will call on them during these times of crisis.

Parents cannot and do not need to do everything for an ill child. It is worthwhile delegating household chores or school lifts. The people around the family and close to the child will want to help. Parents should be reminded that they need to look after their own wellbeing in order to be able to look after their child. Your job is to parent your child, a job which you have been doing from the day they were born.

When a child is diagnosed with a chronic illness, you can feel that your identity is undermined. You become the parent of the sick child. You may feel marked out or different. The most effective way of combating these feelings is to inform those around the family of the condition. Share your newly gained knowledge and, in doing so, you will help those around you to know how best to react and interact with you and your family. Encourage your child to explain their condition to their friends. Remember they will feel isolated from their peer groups and will need a lot of support. Friendships and peer groups are essential for a child to develop a sense of social belonging. It is worth helping your child to communicate their condition to their friends to prevent teasing or bullying. If the child feels comfortable stating why they are different or why they have certain limitations, they will be equipped to deal with the inevitable questions.

When outsiders inevitably ask 'How do you cope?', it is worth taking the time to explain that, in order to be the best parent possible to your child, you have no choice but to cope. Remember that outsiders who say the wrong thing do not mean to hurt you. One care worker who supported families with children that were chronically ill said:

> From what I have seen there is no option, you just get on with it. What makes the journey easier is if there is support. Parents hold themselves together, they can't afford to get ill or think too much, but when the crisis period is over they fall apart.

Exceptional parenting is about putting the needs of your child first and foremost. When faced with a devastating diagnosis, it is tempting to allow the feelings of self-pity to engulf. Remember it is the child who is facing the prognosis head on. They have *no* choice. To be an exceptional parent, you have to adopt the same stance – *I will cope because I have to, I have no choice.* Acceptance is not surrender; instead, it is part of the long process of dealing with the illness. If you do not accept your new reality, you will not be well equipped to meet the challenges ahead.

To assert that there are definitive strategies for coping would be to deny the individual experience of chronic illness. Families react differently to the ongoing demands. While we cannot strategize for every eventuality and for every personality, we can identify needs and provide solutions to meet them.

It is clear that one of the most effective means of coping is to resume a sense of normality. Family life dictates that parents return to work, siblings attend school and the ill child's needs are met and incorporated into family routines. Chronic illness, while having a devastating impact on the child and the family, does not need to engulf family life and threaten social interaction and identity. If attempts to normalize the illness are extreme, then the strategy of normalization will impede coping. There is a balance to be found. To encourage the child to participate in household tasks and regular school life may be appropriate. In fact, enabling the child to feel useful and valued within the family unit is positive. However, extreme normalization as in conducting life as if nothing is different can create problems. Some parents try to live as if the diagnosis has no impact on their quality of life.

Parents should nurture the idea that, while physically limited or ill, the child's self-worth is more than the sum of fully functioning body parts. Apply this to yourself – you are more than the mother or father of a sick child.

The acute anxiety experienced at the time of diagnosis does diminish. To cope with anxiety, it is useful for parents to learn to think in small steps, try not to look at the bigger picture and deal with each individual task at hand. There is nothing to be gained in allowing yourself to be overwhelmed by the 'what ifs'. Tackle tasks that you can control, and do not allow yourself to assume responsibility for everything. Your perspective on life changes radically. Diagnosis of chronic illness creates a new dynamic within the family. Relationships are altered but often strengthened. Families need to take time to explore the impact of the illness on the whole family, talk about how they feel about the diagnosis and reassess hopes for the future.

❖ Advice and action points ❖

- *Listen* to the information being given by the health professionals; take notes and list any concerns you may want to raise at a later opportunity.

- *Ask* questions; do not be afraid to voice your fears and concerns. Never feel that your question is too trivial – ask yourself, 'Is this important to my child?' Remember you are the expert on your child but the doctor is the expert on the illness. Remember the medics have been studying medicine for many years – you are the novice and no one will expect you to understand the condition overnight.

- *Research, research, research*; doctors sometimes advise against trawling the internet for information for fear that we are misled, but ultimately the more information you gather the better prepared you are. Sometimes you have to know a certain amount in order to know which questions to ask.

- *Demand* that the doctor treats the child not just the symptoms. Encourage a relationship between the child and the medical team: allow the child to speak for themselves and interact with their medics.

- *Communicate* with each other within the family unit. Nurture a good working relationship with the medical team through effective communication. The more the medics learn about the whole family, the better equipped they are to provide a more holistic approach to care plans and treatment packages. Learn to communicate with yourself – identify your emotions and learn to express them. Often talking about frustrations or worries helps to lessen them or put them into perspective.

- *Acceptance* is not surrender. Through accepting the diagnosis, you are beginning the process of actively dealing with both the diagnosis and prognosis.

- *Identify* key concerns and discuss with your partner and the medical team how to address them. Discuss treatment options, the benefits and side-effects and what to expect.

- *Discuss* as a family ways in which to support and help each other.

- *Recognize* individual strengths and weaknesses, and assign key tasks with these in mind. For instance, one parent may feel more competent dealing with the practical day-to-day concerns, while the other parent attends hospital appointments.

- *Work* at developing a positive relationship with the medical team. Aim to create a flexible, family-friendly protocol for treatment.

- *Assess* everyday demands and examine ways in which to reduce or eliminate them. Delegate chores to family and friends.

- *Share* information among family members and be open about your need for practical support.

- *Identify* challenges – both large demands and small everyday concerns. This will enable you to plan effectively.

- *Allow* for a period of adjustment. Recognize that not all family members will adjust at the same rate. Some will be ready to cope earlier than others. This also applies to the child with the chronic illness – allow for them, too, to adjust to the diagnosis.

You are now better equipped to deal with the problems that may arise. You have an understanding of your child's condition and their immediate needs. This is the beginning of your journey of parenting through chronic illness.

2

Coping with Hospital and Treatment

The child with chronic illness is first and foremost a child. Their condition may limit them or require treatment, but they are a child first and a patient second.

Most chronic illnesses are managed not cured, and in order to manage them treatment is required. Once the child becomes part of the hospital environment, it is easy for them to feel like a patient. Medics are used to looking at anatomy, dealing with symptoms, diagnoses and prognoses, and prescribing drugs and treatment protocols.

Behind the symptoms is a child or young person. Sometimes the child's voice needs to be amplified above that of the medical profession. Often the parent's role within the hospital setting is to be an advocate, speaking on behalf of their child's needs.

The turmoil of the diagnosis period is often replaced with swift action and the introduction of treatment protocols and care plans; even surgery or further investigations may be required. Learning about the illness or condition only begins after diagnosis. It is likely that a new group of medics is introduced to the family at this stage. Continuity of care can be lost while the child is moved from one hospital department to another. Often this is necessary at the beginning as the diagnosis and treatment needs are discovered.

Following the diagnosis period, parents begin the process of learning about their child's condition and the impact it will have on their life. They also discover treatment options and care plans. Hospital stays may become an ongoing, regular fixture of family life. An entire team of health professionals is involved in looking after one child's case. This team will consist of doctors, nurses, social workers, psychologists, phlebotomists and physiotherapists among others. The team of health professionals will extend into the community with practitioners such as GPs, community nurses and occupational therapists providing support away from the hospital. This wide group of doctors and health professionals will be responsible for the child's long-term treatment and care.

It is important for the parents to establish themselves as active participants in their child's care team. Health professionals acknowledge that, while they are the experts on the condition or disease and its treatment, the parent is the expert on the child. There needs to be an integrated approach, incorporating primary health service treatment providers, and psychological support along with education and social provision. At the centre of this is the family.

Many parents employ control as a coping strategy.[1] They try to obtain information, research the condition thoroughly, talk to others undergoing the same experience and challenge the medics, sometimes seeking second opinions. In learning as much as possible about the condition and the treatment, the parents are being proactive. By focusing on action rather than feeling overwhelmed and unable to help the child, the parents are employing a positive coping strategy. Others find that they enter a phase of denial and cannot accept the prognosis. Their experience of hospital stays is negative and their coping with treatment is inhibited by their inability to be active and become involved in their child's healthcare.

Understanding the child's fears and concerns is as important as learning about the symptoms and physical problems. The parent is often the interpreter or the intermediary – communicating on the child's behalf. The parent's role as part of the healthcare team is significant. Their input is vital and can make a huge difference. How they interpret their role and carry out their care has an impact on the child. The parent can also influence the medical team's performance. Through good communication, conveying the child's needs, the parents can affect how the medics design the care plan and carry out treatment.

Likewise, the medical team are dependent on the parents to implement treatment. Often treatment extends into the child's home life and, without the support of the parents, will not be carried out properly and will eventually fail. The success of treatment is often dependent on how well the parents understand the importance to be organized, disciplined and compliant with treatment.[2] To ensure that the family copes and functions well, they need adequate support from the health professionals.

Family-centred care provides a framework to make sure that the whole family unit is acknowledged. An inclusive, collaborative approach encourages resilience and strength, enabling the family to support each other and pre-empt the need for outside intervention.[3]

Health professionals can positively influence the coping ability of the family through providing information and ongoing communication, and incorporating the needs of each individual family member into their care plan. While all individuals and families cope in different ways and have differing strengths, they can all be successful in their care of the child with a chronic illness if they have encouragement and support. Health professionals need to be aware of the family's innate strengths and respect their cultural differences.[4]

Parents of a child living with autism are often required to follow strict regimes to reinforce learning and behavioural strategies, sometimes adopting gluten- and casein-free diets. Children living with eczema require several lotions and ointments applied daily, and during times of flare-ups are wet wrapped in bandages at night. This can be a tiresome process, made even more difficult when the child protests. For this reason, understanding the treatment and the benefits of carrying out often demanding long-term care is essential. When parents are involved in the child's care plan with the medics and have a thorough understanding of the treatment and its expected impact, then they are more likely to see that the treatment is carried out.

Adherence can refer to attending hospital appointments, enforcing a restricted diet, carrying out physiotherapies, administering medicines or enforcing isolation. It can be difficult for a parent to follow strict adherence, especially if the treatment is to take place over a long period of time and is restrictive and complex. Individual personalities, family stability and support, and good communication with health professionals can be determining features of whether or not compliance with treatment is successful.

The relationship between the medics and the parents is complex and interdependent. At times, there will be conflicts and communication will be strained but, ultimately, both parties have the welfare of the child in mind. Health professionals need to have an understanding of the problems or issues as seen by the parents, and to be active in listening to their views. For support to be effective, it must be appropriate, timely and relevant. Dr Anthony McCarthy understands the need for parents and medics to work together:

> There is no doubt that the parents are and should always be regarded as part of the child's care team. In fact they are by far the main players and the medical professionals are very much minor players in this team. There will however be times when the parents and medical professionals' opinions differ. In my experience most differences of opinion usually come from miscommunication and therefore further dialogue quite often sorts this out.

One of the greatest concerns facing parents with regards to treatment is prognosis, especially if the outcome of treatment is not fully known. Uncertainty about the benefits of potentially harmful treatment is a real cause for concern. The side-effects of neurosurgery can result in damaging the child, mentally and physically, or, worse, the child could die in surgery or through post-operative complications. Likewise, the side-effects of chemotherapy are substantial: hair loss, nausea, bone marrow repression and risk of infection all have to be weighed up against the long-term prognosis of the cancer and the probability of death. Radiotherapy to treat a brain tumour can be life saving but render the child intellectually challenged. Parents are forced to make life and death decisions for their children. These decisions need to be made with as much knowledge as possible. It is important that the health professionals, while supporting the parents, provide them with information to make informed choices.

One of the best pieces of advice I was given at the beginning of my son's treatment was to keep a diary. The object of the diary was to record hospital appointment times, treatment periods and blood results. In keeping records, I was able to anticipate the effect of certain drugs, to identify when Owen's blood counts were likely to be low and to have a clear overview of how he was coping with treatment. Being organized in this way gave me a sense of control and enabled me to be informed about Owen's wellbeing from one clinic appointment to the next. I needed to stay informed and to remember his reactions to each cycle of chemotherapy in order to provide the consultant with the information he needed about how Owen was responding and coping with treatment. Certain drug cocktails would make him extremely sick; others made his joints ache and caused headaches. Keeping records of how his blood count level responded to the chemotherapy enabled me to anticipate when his white cell count would be too low to risk catching infections, and I could therefore avoid taking him into crowded areas.

It is also useful to take notes during hospital appointments. Jotting down key words and phrases allows the parent to take in the information and the terminology. It is all too easy to sit in front of a consultant listening to but not absorbing the information. Parents can feel uneasy questioning medical professionals and try to avoid looking stupid by not asking them to clarify certain information. It is important for the parent to realize that the consultant has spent many years studying medicine to come to this point. They are the experts and they do not expect you to have the same knowledge base that they have. They are open to being questioned and are willing to help you become better informed.

Following the diagnosis of chronic illness, hospital stays and regular clinic appointments often dominate everyday life. The family unit is put under enormous strain, particularly if the hospital is not within easy travelling distance. Some hospitals and connected charities provide living accommodation for the whole family close to the hospital, but work commitments and schooling for siblings often dictate that the family is separated for varying periods of time. Communication is vital when this separation occurs. Anxieties mount if the siblings are not informed about the sick child or when the parents will return. A sense of abandonment can develop out of this resentment. Dr McCarthy recognizes the strain families are put under during long hospital stays: 'Prolonged hospital stays cause disruption not only to the parent and the child but also to the partner and other siblings at home. These are often regarded as the forgotten casualties.'

Why certain families cope with chronic illness better than others is not clear. It is clear that how effectively a family communicates and how well they are supported has an impact on their coping ability. The severity of the condition and the likelihood of death have a greater psychological impact. Difficulties in coping arise when the child is in pain, or the illness is particularly severe in its symptoms. People will revert to personality type. A resilient person is likely to cope better than someone with a history of depression.[5]

We all have inbuilt coping mechanisms, some more advanced than others. This is not to say that the parent can opt out, claiming they are not strong enough to cope. We all have reserves of strength that we do not recognize in ourselves until we are put under extreme stress.

Treatment is offered to children with a chronic illness to alleviate symptoms and, where possible, to halt the worsening progression of the condition. How a child copes with the treatment is dependent on the nature and severity of the condition, the child's personality and their family support. Studies have also found that during periods of crisis and stress the child does not cope as well with their condition. It is therefore of paramount importance for the hospital system to be supportive of the whole family in order to reduce stress for the child. Support should be on both emotional and practical levels.

Collaboration between the team of health professionals and the family enhances the hospital experience. It is good practice for the medical team to work in a multi-disciplined way. For instance, in Cardiff where Owen was diagnosed and first treated, his neurosurgeon and neurology team met on a regular basis with his oncologist and radiotherapist, even though radiology in the initial phase was not an option for treatment. They all maintained an active interest in his progress and attended clinic appointments on an alternate rota to see him. They were all experts in their own fields and could each offer a different dimension to the overall care package. This multi-disciplined approach allows for a more effective strategy when it comes to determining treatment.

The interdependence and shared approach between medics should also cascade down to nursing teams, play therapists, occupational therapists and community practitioners. This enhances the overall wellbeing of the child and ensures a more holistic approach.

Children living with cystic fibrosis require a care team including a pulmonologist, nurses, doctors, dieticians, respiratory therapists, physical therapists, gastroenterologists, diabetologists and psychologists. If each of these medical specialists treats the child without collaboration, then it can be detrimental to the child's wellbeing. Care for the child with a chronic illness requires team effort.

Collaboration is important for dealing with chronic illness because of the long-term nature of the condition. Over a period of time, it is likely that the child will move on within the health system. As a child grows and develops, the condition may change and affect them in different ways. The multi-disciplined approach allows the child and their parents to become familiar with a health professional before they are being actively treated by them, thus allowing for a greater sense of continuity. Knowing that a doctor who may have to treat your child in the future has already fostered an interest in the case is reassuring. Interaction between the family and the wider medical team promotes a more positive attitude.

However, with a diverse and interdependent approach, it is also worth noting that leadership should be clearly established. All the medical team are accountable, but key managerial responsibility should lie with one particular leader. This sense of ownership with one person ensures that there is co-ordination of the shared goals. The parents need to have one individual whom they know they can approach with concerns, and one key person to rely on to navigate the system. For a collective multi-disciplinary approach to work, there must be a clear structure of what is expected of each individual.

In many hospitals, this sharing of information and experience extends to other geographical regions. The internet has made contact with other consultants readily accessible. No one should work alone. In some rare cases, a doctor may only come across a particular illness once or twice in their careers, and to be able to link in with other professionals who have more experience is of great value. This global interdependence means that accessing a second opinion is easier, providing a more comprehensive view of how to progress with treatment.

A multi-disciplined approach is not always realistic. Constraints on time, budgets and even geography can mean that a child does not meet a health professional before they are being referred for specific treatment. People move on from positions and new people will inevitably come along. This can be positive in that new people can have a different approach, a fresh take on a situation or experience of a different way of working. The main principle in ensuring a successful ongoing relationship with the medical team and between the health professionals is to treat every relationship as if it will be long term and have an impact on the child.

In some cases, treatment will be experimental. More children with cancer take part in clinical trials than adults. A clinical trial involves the study of new drugs and therapies and how they are administered. The treatment protocol will be the same for all patients within a certain category, dependent on type of cancer, grade of tumour, age, etc. Clinical trials have accelerated the rate of cure for some cancers in contributing to scientific research. Progress is dependent on developing our knowledge of how the disease reacts to certain drugs and conditions.

Informed consent from the parents is required before a child or young person can be enrolled in a clinical trial. This means that the medical team have discussed at length all available treatment options with the parents; that treatments available at other hospitals have been investigated; that the medics have provided the family with the pros and cons; and that the family feel comfortable with their decision. Often a clinical trial is the best hope for cure or long-term management and parents feel they have no choice but to enrol their child. Balancing the impact of treatment on the child with quality of life is often a primary consideration for parents.

The child's view of hospital

The enormity of coping with a chronic illness is often overwhelming for the child. They think in small segments – the here and now, how they are affected in the present by the condition. Hospital can become the physical manifestation of their condition. They can associate their illness with hospital and feel resentful towards the hospital if they do not understand that the medics' role is to help them.

Hospitals can be intimidating places. Many hospitals allocate budgets to decorate wards with child-friendly designs and colourful murals. The equipment, sounds and smells will all be alien to a child and can be threatening. This strange environment takes its toll and can exacerbate a child's anxiety. This is apart from the often painful procedures a child may have to undergo as part of their treatment. Blood tests, scans and surgery can all become routine but no less intrusive and painful.

Hospital stays fill most people with trepidation. Often our preconceived ideas of what hospital is like are passed on to our children. If a parent is anxious about needles, then the child will inevitably have the same apprehensions unless the parent makes a conscious effort to hide or overcome their fear.

Parents should be encouraged to stay with their child while in hospital. Often camp beds are provided but many parents spend nights trying to sleep on chairs. My husband, Liam, and I spent weeks at Owen's bedside sleeping on armchairs. There is a support community between parents who stay on the wards.

Dr Arun Mathews, national director of research and medical education for a nationwide hospitalist group called the Apogee Medical Group, believes that it is important for parents to feel welcome on hospital wards: 'Children's hospitals have come a long way from the "closed unit" approach, allowing flexible visiting hours, overnight lodging, etc. for families dealing with a sick child.'

In some hospitals, child life specialists work with families to support them during their hospital stay. Their role is to help children cope with their fears and anxieties, and to adjust to the diagnosis. They can also inform the medics of psychosocial or cultural issues that may affect the child, and they can advocate on the child's behalf. Like play therapists, child life specialists can provide preparation for medical procedures and support for the child through play. This play therapy and support can take place at home before the child even attends hospital, or at the hospital bedside.

Dr Mathews has found through his research for Hospital-based Online Pediatric Environment (HOPE) that 'role-play, gaming, education and preparation are key factors in reducing the stress and anxiety of a paediatric hospitalization'.

It is important to be as honest as possible with the child about hospital stays. The child needs to have an understanding of why the hospital stay is necessary. Explanations of treatment and procedures need to be in age-appropriate terms. If the child is encouraged to feel that the medical team is working to help them, they are more likely to feel at ease and to co-operate. The parent should try to use encouraging language when talking about the medics. The doctors and nurses should also introduce themselves to the child and use first names to keep the relationship informal.

Chronic illness often entails regular periods of hospitalization and it is natural for parents to feel resentful and full of dread. If the parents are positive about hospital stays, then the child will be more likely to cope. The parents should help the child focus on the nicer aspects of being in hospital: for instance, they will meet new friends, possibly see friends they have met on other hospital appointments, play with different toys and take part in play therapy activities. Explain why the child needs to go to hospital, give an estimated time for the hospital stay and talk about returning home. Most paediatric wards encourage parents to stay overnight. If this is not encouraged, the parent should try to negotiate staying or at least being in a parents' room nearby.

At the time of diagnosis, the parent learns about the condition, what it entails and what it means for their child's future. When treatment is an option, for either cure or maintenance of a condition, the learning becomes about medical procedures, treatment and medicines. In learning about the treatment, the parent will be better prepared for how the child will be affected. They will also be better equipped for explaining the treatment and procedures to the child and, in doing so, help ease their anxieties.

To help the child adjust to staying in hospital and dealing with treatment, the parent must talk to the child about their illness. In being open and honest in age-appropriate terms, the parent can help the child to feel safe and secure.

Coping with pain

Many children with a chronic illness will experience pain at some time in their lives. Pain can result from their condition as in juvenile rheumatoid arthritis or muscular dystrophy, brain tumours or head injury, or it can be the result of treatment or hospital procedures. Some children live with chronic pain – that is, pain that is persistent and lasting – while others experience periods of acute pain that can be easily treated and do not last for long, or are the result of procedural activity. Acute pain usually disappears when an injury has healed. However, chronic pain is long lasting.

Procedural pain is often traumatic for a child. The fear and anxiety associated with procedural pain can be minimized if the child and the parents are fully prepared for the intervention. It is important that difficult procedures are carried out by experienced medics to prevent the child enduring the procedure more than once if it is not successful the first time. The child should not have to endure more than one painful procedure at a time. Medics should try to schedule injections, blood tests or lumbar punctures at separate times to prevent the child becoming traumatized and over-anxious. If the child understands the procedure, they are more likely to co-operate and cope with the procedural pain.

Sometimes acute pain, as in the incident of a head injury, can lead to chronic pain. Parents caring for a child living with chronic pain feel helpless, guilty and distressed. It can be frustrating when the medics appear to dismiss chronic pain or expect the child to live with it. This does not have to be the case. There have been advances in research into paediatric chronic pain and medics can offer many forms of pain management and treatment.

It can be easy for the child to blame the medics for their pain, illness or disability. They associate hospital with their condition, so it is necessary to nurture a good relationship with the hospital staff. With this in mind, it is worth trying to make hospital appointments and stays as pleasant as possible. Many parents find that bringing special toys to hospital, and even the child's pillow from home, can give them a sense of comfort and security.

Managing pain is essential for the child's wellbeing. Unfortunately, some children live with chronic pain and suffer sometimes needlessly. Identifying pain and the severity of it, and describing it effectively, involves good communication. Infants and young children do not have the capacity to communicate their pain levels. Parents learn to interpret the child's pain.

Most pain should be treated and dealt with through the use of analgesics. There is a range of psychological, physical and pharmaceutical advancements to help relieve pain in children. However, there has been an unfortunate history of pain in children being under-estimated and medics believing that infants and young children do not feel pain as much as adults. There has also been a belief that opiates are harmful for children and are therefore restricted in use.[6]

When children are prescribed any drug, it is necessary to enquire about potential side-effects. Parents need to understand how a drug will affect a child and to be aware of harmful risks. Medication is not the only solution to pain management, but the use of drugs should not be overlooked for chronic pain in children.

Parents should try to identify, along with the child, warning signals that pain is approaching, in order to provide time to react and be prepared. If the child is outside the family home and they recognize fatigue or cramp or a headache as a precursor to the onset of pain, then the family can return home to access medication or provide a quiet, softly lit room. Often familiar surroundings and comfort can help the child cope with pain.

The medical profession has a responsibility for countering pain in children. There needs to be improvements in clinical practice to ensure that current research is translated into action so that children do not suffer needlessly. Often children and young people living with conditions such as sickle cell anaemia, neuromuscular conditions and some cancers are not assessed appropriately for pain relief. Their pain is often underestimated and debilitating, affecting their quality of life substantially.

Following neurosurgery, Owen spent several days with a drain coming out of his skull. It was vital to keep him at one level in order to keep the drain running smoothly and to prevent it coming out. Postoperatively, he suffered severe headaches. At one stage, he was rolling on the bed in agony while I tried desperately to hold him down for fear that the drain would be dislodged. The nursing staff refused to give him pain relief because his next dose was not due for a further hour. They also wanted to keep him conscious to assess his recovery.

This was one of the few occasions when dealing with medics that we had to be assertive and demand action. I demanded to see the on-call doctor – who took one look at Owen and ordered the nurse to give him the necessary medication. Nursing staff have to adhere to strict guidelines when administering medication for fear of overdosing a patient, but the lack of flexibility and common sense caused Owen to suffer unnecessarily. There has to be some way of responding to a child's needs before the pain becomes unbearable. Owen should not have suffered; the risks of the medication being administered early should have been taken to ease his immense pain. The nurses should have responded to the evidence of

Owen's pain rather than asserting that he should not require pain relief for a further hour.

In 'No pain – all gain: advocating for improved paediatric pain management',[7] Stinson and McGrath state: 'The under treatment of pain in children can no longer be attributed to a lack of research evidence, but rather to our inability to use what we know in our everyday practices.'

Recognizing and communicating pain in children often falls to the parents. They are the child's advocates and their ability to communicate well with the child and with the health professionals can influence the level and quality of pain management the child receives. Parents need to be able to identify symptoms and respond to their child's needs, assessing their pain level and making judgements as to whether or not they are receiving adequate pain management. Responsibility for educating and informing the parents about pain and its management lies with the health professionals. They must endeavour to empower parents to recognize pain and to respond when necessary. Like so much involving chronic illness, pain management requires collaboration between the child, the parents and the medics.

Many chronic conditions can cause pain: juvenile rheumatoid arthritis, muscular dystrophy, cystic fibrosis and some cancers, to name just some. In many chronic conditions, the management of pain is complex and problematic.

For children living with cancer, the pain can result from the tumour mass itself, effect of invasive procedures, therapy, inflammation caused by infection, tissue distention or other causes related to the treatment. Chemotherapy has many side-effects; nausea and hair loss are well known, but the chemotherapy agents can also cause problems with joint pain, headaches and abdominal pain. Radiotherapy causes skin irritation like sunburn, headaches and nausea, while cancer patients routinely have blood tests, veins accessed for treatment to be administered and lumbar punctures.

Pain can have a damaging effect on a child's ability to cope with their condition. While pain can cause stress, stress in itself can exacerbate pain. Family problems, worries about school and fear of hospitalization can all induce stress in the child with a chronic illness. A child living with irritable bowel syndrome is likely to experience symptoms during times of stress. Problems concerning pain management often emerge when the child is being cared for at home. Inadequate community healthcare provision can result in children's and young people's pain relief needs being overlooked or unidentified.

If a child is to undergo a painful procedure, while not dwelling on the anticipation of pain, it is necessary for the parent to be honest. Explain why the procedure is necessary and how the medics will try to minimize the soreness. The child needs to know that you trust the medics and that you approve of the procedure. Use language that is appropriate to the age of the child. Tell them that they will feel a sting, some discomfort, an ache, a twinge, a smarting or a throbbing. These terms are more descriptive than simply saying 'pain', and suggest degrees of painfulness. A gauge of the levels of pain is useful for determining how bad a procedure will be. Some hospitals use a smiley face chart with the faces progressing from crying to frowning to laughing to assist in determining pain relief. The younger child can relate to a visual image to describe how they feel, while an older child can give an indication on a scale of one to ten.

Research has shown that children who are more anxious before surgery experience more pain during their hospital stay and at home. These children, as assessed by their parents, experienced more post-operative pain and sleep problems.[8]

Dr Arun Mathews has experience of using video games on paediatric wards and recognizes the use of gaming as an adjunct for the management of anxiety associated with surgery. He referred to one particular study wherein:

> The research group gave kids about to undergo surgery in the pre-op setting handheld gaming devices, and noted a drop in self-reported anxiety levels… A paediatrician in Texas by the name of Hofmann, managing a burn unit, also demonstrated that gaming could decrease the need for opiate analgesia in burn patients undergoing painful dressing changes and wound debridements.

Pain management is not solely concerned with pharmacological intervention or physical therapy: it requires preparation and good communication to enable a child to feel comfortable and relaxed about the procedure or surgery that will cause the pain.

While being open and honest about painful procedures, it is also worth noting that some children will not respond positively to being told a lot of detail. Fear of a procedure can be worse than the actual reality and explaining too much or labouring a point can make a child over-anxious and refuse to allow the medics near them. If this happens, it is best to remove the child from the situation until they are calm and more willing to be co-operative. If possible, the child should be given realistic choices – for instance, where an injection is sited, which arm is used when taking blood, if medicine is in liquid or tablet form. These choices allow the child to feel a degree of control. When choice is limited, let the child decide which hand the parent holds or where they sit to have the procedure done.

Talking about positive, happy experiences during uncomfortable procedures is an effective distraction. Visualization or guided imagery techniques have been used for centuries in pain management. Carrying out visualization techniques effectively takes time and practice. It is worth practising the techniques with the child before hospital procedures begin. High levels of stress can be combated through recalling pleasant sights, sounds and smells. The child can be encouraged to focus on a happy memory – perhaps a trip to the beach or the countryside – and in a slow, low voice the parent can help the child revisit the place in their mind by describing what they saw and what they did. Visualization can also be effective in controlling nausea caused by chemotherapy. It can be practised in hospital or at home, and used to help alleviate pain and anxiety.

Often when a child is in pain or distress, they hold their breath and tense their body. This tension in the muscles exacerbates pain. The parent should encourage the child to exhale forcefully and to breathe in slowly and regularly. Parents can also benefit from breathing techniques and visualization to help them cope with stress.

Massage, hydrotherapy, hypnotherapy and acupuncture can all be employed to help with chronic pain. However, it is necessary to talk to your physician before undertaking any complementary therapies that may interfere with conventional treatments.

Distraction is often the most effective remedy for pain. Most children's wards are equipped with toys and craft materials and, by allowing the child to become absorbed in such an activity (play therapists are useful in these situations), the parent or medic can slowly begin talking about what the doctors or nurses need to do. It is always necessary to gain the child's trust, to enable them to feel in control. Allow them as far as possible to say when they are ready to undergo the procedure. Forcibly holding a child to undergo a blood test or an injection is traumatic and damaging to their relationship with their health professionals.

The hospital experience

Health professionals have a responsibility to ensure that the child's hospital experience is as positive as possible. Paediatric wards should be well equipped with toys, books, DVDs and the latest digital equipment for video games. As Dr Arun Mathews asserts:

> I suppose when we get down to the nuts and bolts of things, there is very little that can take away from the seriousness of childhood illness.
>
> Interactive digital entertainment can help alleviate the misery of a hospital stay, either by providing a stimulating distraction or allowing children of like-minded interests to play together. These experiences need not necessarily be 'directly relevant' or 'educational' in order to be effective.

Medical equipment can be a source of interest to the child and it is useful to allow them to learn about the doctor's 'tools'. Familiarity will ease their concern. Teaching a child the correct terminology for procedures and hospital equipment also helps to take the mystique out of the situation when they are hearing terms and jargon they do not understand.

Our use of language can determine how the child interprets their condition. It is helpful if you have gathered your own information if possible before giving an explanation. The way in which you convey information to your child about the condition and treatment can determine how they feel about it. If you can speak in positive terms and with confidence about the medical profession, then your child will feel secure and more open to trusting the staff and the procedures.

The parents and medical team need to win the child's trust and, by being less than truthful, the child will soon learn that they cannot feel secure and trusting. Remember, to the child, terms such as 'cancer' or 'tumour' are not frightening until we give them negative associations. Pejorative terms like 'bad cells' are more likely to create a sense of wrongness and even suggest that the child is in some way bad. Likewise, attributing blame or describing a genetic condition as being linked to a parent creates a sense of wrongness or blame within the child. If a parent chooses to speak about the child's illness in cloaked language, it is not protecting the child – sooner or later, the child will overhear others talking about their condition; they may then be frightened to discover that they are being shielded and naturally assume the worst.

Looking at the hospital environment from the child's perspective is illuminating. When a child has been diagnosed as chronically ill, they will probably have been subjected to a barrage of tests. From their viewpoint, they have been accosted by large people in white coats with strange instruments. Sometimes these people have caused them pain. Worse still, their parents have held them while these procedures have occurred. Put bluntly in these terms, we can understand the child who refuses to co-operate. When a child has endured a chronic illness, they are often limited in their physical or mental abilities and can be aware that their peers do not experience the same limitations. One of the main ways in which they can control what is happening to them is through refusing to take medicine or work with the medical team.

While trying to convey a positive, upbeat attitude, it is helpful if you also allow your child to express their fears and concerns. The child should be reassured that it is normal to have concerns and worries, and that it is permissible to cry. They should be able to acknowledge their anxieties and talk them through. Just as a parent can try to shelter a child from their worries, so too can the child. A child may not speak directly about their worries but instead manifest their concerns by withdrawing or even misbehaving. Sometimes it is difficult for the child to understand their own fears and to express them.

Displays of negativity and despair will only heighten a child's anxieties. While hospital stays are draining and undergoing treatment is difficult for the child, the parent should project a positive attitude, interpreting the hospital stays as necessary to improve the child's condition. Learning about the medical procedures, the medicines and side-effects, and knowing the signs of emergencies and how to deal with them, also lessens a parent's anxiety. A sense of control on the parent's part is reassuring to the child. If the parent appears to be coping with the hospital and treatment demands, then the child will feel more secure and reassured. The child learns from the parent how to cope with their illness and how best to deal with symptoms and treatment.

The most effective way for a parent to eliminate their own fears is to become informed and to take control of the child's condition. The medical team should make time to inform parents about their child's condition and treatments. Some hospitals employ education nurses who provide parents with information. The parent should not be afraid to ask questions. In order to become more confident in dealing with the condition, a parent needs to become something of an expert on the illness. This does not happen overnight. A sense of control develops over time, and can dip and waver according to circumstance. Managing chronic illness requires dedication and long-term commitment.

The need for information varies from parent to parent. Some parents immerse themselves in researching their child's condition while others resist knowledge for fear of learning distressing news. The extent of the need for parents to be involved and manage their child's care depends on the demands of the condition. Parents need to be guided and directed by the health professionals to learn how much involvement is required. The clinicians should if possible provide literature at the time of diagnosis for the parents to have information to consider. Parents should ask for direction as to where to go to find more information. Doctors will be able to recommend to the parents good internet sites, journals and books.

The internet has vastly changed access to information. Prior to internet access, parents would have to trawl through medical text books in science libraries to gain information. Now the research is more accessible and instant. Parents with computers can become experts on their child's condition without leaving home. The internet also enables parents to make contact with health professionals overseas, thereby reaching other, more distant, experts in their fields. Second opinions are no longer confined to the hospital the child is attending. Contact with other families experiencing the same chronic illness is also made possible via the internet. Many charities and voluntary groups host online forums for parents to share information and support each other.

While undergoing treatment and dealing with hospital stays is difficult for the child, side-effects arising from the treatment can also cause anxiety. Body image and side-effects of treatment can cause psychological and emotional problems for the child with a chronic illness. Surgery can leave scars, drugs can cause weight gain or loss and the illness itself can cause physical deformities or distortion. Children and young people undergoing chemotherapy treatment may have to endure hair loss. Some conditions can cause short stature and delay of puberty, which can lead to negative self-image.

Self-esteem can be damaged if a child feels 'different'. An altered appearance may also raise questions from peers and others. The child needs to be informed about their condition in order to be able to address teasing or bullying. It is worth speaking to teachers to inform and educate the children who come into contact with the child with a chronic illness to prevent issues of ignorance. If the child has the opportunity to make friends on the hospital ward with other children in the same position, it will enhance their self-esteem. Children on oncology wards are relaxed about their bald heads but often choose to wear hats when going out to avoid drawing attention to themselves.

Parents need to feel that they can beneficially influence events and their outcomes through their efforts. Passivity may create a victim-like attitude and be detrimental to the overall coping ability of the family. The parent may not be able to cure a child but, in many instances, through their dedication they can enhance the child's wellbeing and, in some cases, prevent unnecessary infections or further hospital stays. Likewise, a child's sense of involvement and control can positively influence their coping ability.

An effective way of dealing with a child who does not want to co-operate with their medical team is to create a sense of responsibility for their self-care.[9] They need to be motivated to stay in hospital and to take medicines or, in the case of cystic fibrosis, spend hours having physiotherapy. This motivation can be induced from the idea that they have ownership over their condition. The medical team can advise the parent on how best to encourage the child to carry out tasks to help themselves. The health professionals should work with the child or young person to help them understand why treatment is necessary. When the child understands the benefits of adhering to treatment, they will be more likely to comply. Parents and medics can discuss with the child how their condition affects them – their self-image, limited movement, disabilities, limited interaction with friends or prolonged absence from school. When the child or young person understands that treatment may help them to resolve some of the limitations caused by their condition, they will be more accepting.

Where possible, children should be encouraged to manage and take control of their condition. A child with asthma can decide when they need to use an inhaler, and a child with diabetes can be aware of when their blood sugar levels may be low. Even very young children can be involved in their care management. Children need to be given choices with regards to their care: can they take a medicine with a particular drink, for instance, or decide which order their medicines are given in? Sometimes a child's ability to choose is limited but even small levels of choice, such as where to sit when an injection is being given, can make all the difference to their sense of control.

The child should be praised for their involvement in their care. Through this sense of responsibility for themselves, they will begin to understand the need to attend clinic appointments, stay in hospital, take medication and have blood tests done.

Encouraging responsibility is also a positive way to build a child's self-confidence and allow them to grow. It is easy to closet a sick child and over-protect them, but this is a great disservice to the child. The extreme parent teaches the child self-reliance and, within safe boundaries, encourages them to grow and reach their potential. To over-protect a child to their detriment is to selfishly fulfil the parent's own need for control. Most children with a chronic illness will say they want normality, to be treated like their siblings and peers.

It is essential to acknowledge and listen to the child's concerns and worries. Many parents want to tell the child not to worry, that there is nothing to be worried about. In adopting an upbeat, almost dismissive attitude, the parent is at risk of alienating the child and preventing them from being open about their fears. Instead, it is helpful if you acknowledge their worries and respond in a caring, considerate manner. Instead of saying 'don't worry', you could say 'I understand, I worry at times too, but you know that the treatment will help…' This acknowledges that we all experience worries but that there is a positive course of action to take.

Medics should be encouraged to address a child personally when they are going to carry out a procedure. It is easy to talk over the child to the parent or staff and be neglectful of the patient. Interaction between the doctor and the child is essential. They have to establish a relationship, and how the child is treated by the medical team can have a huge effect on how they cope with their illness. The child deserves respect.

I can remember being astounded when talking to a nurse about why she worked on the high-dependency paediatric ward; she told me she preferred working with sick children because they were often too ill to complain or demand. Her attitude is thankfully not the norm, but it made me realize how vulnerable sick children really are when they cannot speak up for themselves.

Treatment for chronic illness often needs to be tailored to the individual child. The healthcare team need to work with the parents when designing a treatment plan. Parents are required to manage and implement their child's treatment. To be effective providers of this care, they need quality training. This training often falls under the remit of nursing staff. Some children need daily injections of insulin, others need medicines or intensive physiotherapy, all of which require the parents to be appropriately trained.

Practical considerations such as the parents' work commitments need to be taken into consideration when planning long-term hospital stays. It is important for the child to have a parent stay with them overnight and, where possible, this should be shared between parents to ease the strain. Single families should try to involve the extended family in treatment and care plans. Grandparents are particularly useful in easing the burden and are often keen to help.

Families who live far from treatment centres face the added burden of travel. Hospital staff should consider the availability of community nurses to administer treatment, or more local hospitals taking responsibility for monitoring or blood work. Conference calling, email and web cams can all be utilized to limit the travel the sick child and their family have to undertake. Unfortunately, strategic thinking, which encourages the use of local treatment centres or GP surgeries to carry out minor tests or blood work, or to administer medication, is overlooked. All too often a child is expected to travel to their main hospital for treatment even though they could be attended to in their own locality. Health professionals need to work with parents to try to address issues of long distance and to look for ways of easing the burden of travelling to and from hospital.

Infants

Babies develop attachment to one or two adults – their parents. Infants with a chronic illness are exposed to numerous people, nurses and doctors who all interact with them. While some infants can cope with wide social interaction, others find it difficult. Separation from the mother for medical procedures can also cause anxiety for the child.

Babies need a lot of stimulation and the hospital environment can be limiting for them. A baby lying in a special care baby unit for days needs to have visual stimulation. Babies explore their world through touch and taste, and parents need to help them have sensory experiences while staying in hospital.

At the same time, babies need reassurance, and the best way to communicate this is through physical contact and play. Music and play are useful distractions during tests or injections. Comforters provide reassurance especially during hospital stays. My son was dependent on one of my satin pyjama tops, and derived much comfort from sleeping with it in the alien hospital environment.

Nutrition for babies and toddlers is of paramount importance and this is increased when there is chronic illness. Sometimes special foods and formulas are prescribed. Breast milk is the best form of nutrition a baby can receive. I can remember seeing a very young baby on the oncology ward breast-feeding while hooked up to an intravenous drip of chemotherapy. The contrast of the mother feeding her infant while the toxic treatment was administered was both shocking and reassuring – that baby was receiving the best possible care from its mother.

Weight and length are often used to determine how well a baby is developing. A normal growth rate will indicate that the child is getting enough food and growing at the expected rate. It is difficult to not feel demoralized when growth is not following the expected curve. The medical team will be aware of the impact of the child's illness on their growth and it is perhaps more necessary to see a progression than an average rate of growth.

Feeding and sleeping patterns can be altered by hospital stays and present challenges to the parents when trying to create a normal routine at home. Babies can experience separation anxiety if parents are forced to leave them in hospital. Separation from parents and sometimes siblings, even for short periods of time, can give rise to problems of security and trust.

A baby's developmental milestones – sitting up, rolling over, crawling, bearing weight on their legs and vocalizing – are all indicators to the health professionals as to how the child is progressing. Chronic illness can interfere with these milestones and impede the child's development. It is easy for the parent to make comparisons with their other children and friends' children of the same age, and then feel demoralized and concerned. While it is important to be able to convey to the medics if the child is limited in their development, it is also worth celebrating the child with a chronic illness's own achievements.

When a young baby is chronically ill, sometimes the parents need to administer injections or forcibly give the child medication. This can be traumatic for the parents and the child. Some parents, and mothers in particular, can find themselves not wanting to be present when a difficult procedure is being carried out, saying that they cannot bear to watch their baby being injected or having blood taken.

As one father described it, 'I felt that my son was being tortured and what made it worse was that I was the one holding him down.' Although this father was disturbed and distraught to see his child undergo painful interventions, he coped with his distress in order to be the one who helped his child with his treatment. The child did not resent the father and turned to him for comfort as soon as the procedure had finished.

The 'extreme' parent thinks of the child first and foremost: will the procedure be worse for the child if the mother or father is out of the room? The child needs to be reassured by its parents. Holding a child during a painful procedure, while being extremely difficult, is an act of love.

However, at times the parent needs to step back if they are too stressed to deal with a certain procedure. If the parent's distress is causing anxiety for the child, it is better for them to be absent. The mother and father can alternate being in the role of hand-holder during painful procedures and even grandparents can step in when necessary.

Identifying the extent of pain in an infant can be difficult. Obvious signs include crying, irritability or stiffness of limbs, but vital signs such as heart rate, breathing rate and the amount of oxygen in the blood are also used to assess pain. Pain in a baby should be treated and managed without hesitation.

Two- to four-year-olds

Toddlers are developing a sense of independence and need to explore their environment. Chronic illness can impede their mobility and limit their ability to explore.

Children of this age group have difficulty understanding their illness and the relationship between the condition and treatment. They are highly imaginative and will benefit from play-acting out hospital scenarios. Talk about special medicine to help them, explain about the role of the doctor and the nurses. Describe the equipment in terms they can relate to and use pictures and books to support the information you are giving them.[10]

To deal with painful or uncomfortable procedures, parents should do some advanced planning. Think about how best to distract the child – a favourite music tape can be played, a previously unseen toy can suddenly be offered, or bubbles blown with the child. Holding the child's hand and helping them to breathe slowly can also help. Most children's wards have stickers proclaiming the child's courage after a procedure. The child will come to anticipate the reward of the sticker.

Children that are chronically ill often become fussy eaters, either because their treatment affects how the food tastes, as in chemotherapy, or they are gaining a sense of control in the one area of their lives where they can assert themselves. Try to be relaxed about meal times and encourage your child to try different foods.

Five- to ten-year-olds

Children in this age group can often refuse to believe they are ill. They cannot understand the limitations imposed on them and can be resentful. The child may react aggressively towards siblings or other children without fully realizing why they are so angry. They can also be angry towards their parents and medics and want to focus blame. Love and reassurance are the best ways to counter anger. The child will feel bewildered and anxious initially, but with patience and understanding they will adjust.

Children in this age group will be able to plan their hospital stay by packing their favourite possessions – books, music tapes and games are all welcome distractions. By encouraging the child to think about what they would like to bring to the ward, the parent is instilling a sense of responsibility in the child. They begin to understand that they will be away from home for a while and that they can have their favourite things with them for comfort and familiarity. Food can be an issue for children of this age and it is worthwhile investigating what kind of food is offered by the hospital. Some units provide cooking areas for parents to make food for children who are regularly in hospital.

Adolescents

Adolescence is a period of uncertainty, change and adjustment for every teenager. An adolescent with a chronic illness faces the added burden of limitations imposed by their condition and dependence on parents at a time when they desire to be independent. It is common for young people to deny they are ill. Conflict between this age group and parents arises as the young person seeks independence at the risk of damaging their health. Parents need to set clear boundaries while enabling the young person to have as much choice and control as possible.

Dr Anthony McCarthy believes that:

> The main difficulty with adolescent patients in particular is that this diagnosis tends to rob them of the essential formative years of their development. They naturally grieve for this loss and they usually blame either their parents or carers for same or perhaps even the medical professionals.

Physical changes in the adolescent with the advent of puberty and hormone changes can affect the chronic condition. A chronic illness may delay puberty and restrict size causing the young person to feel different from their peers.

Problems of non-compliance (where the young person refuses medication or avoids doing anything that will help their condition/illness) can be a problem for adolescents as they adjust to accepting their illness. Adolescents try to assert their independence through non-compliance.

Parents and medics should work together to help the adolescent understand their illness and treatment. If the young person has a good understanding of their condition, how it affects them and the need for treatment, they will be more willing to co-operate.[11]

Young people need to be involved in decision making. They can negotiate and agree treatment and care plans and will then be more likely to take an active interest in implementing them. The young person needs to understand fully the side-effects of drugs. When side-effects occur, it is less worrying to know that they are caused by the medication rather than the condition.

Care teams need to show a degree of flexibility in working with adolescents – for example, can drugs be administered at night rather than during the school day?

Some young people may refuse experimental treatment. They may choose to live a limited life unhampered by hospitals and medication. Young people of this age are considered old enough to make decisions of this nature, although it is extremely difficult for parents when conflict of this nature arises. Life-supporting treatment can be gruelling, especially dialysis or chemotherapy. The young person may take the view that they would rather have quality of life than longevity.

Involving young people in their treatment and care plans empowers them and gives them a sense of control. Pamela Hinds, head of nursing research at St Jude Children's Research Hospital, was the lead author of a study that appeared in an online issue of the *Journal of Clinical Oncology*. Hinds *et al.* set out to understand more about the patients themselves and their attitudes.[12]

The study followed 20 terminally ill children between 10 and 20 years old to discover how much they understood about their illness and how much they could participate in their own care. It was discovered that, instead of feeling burdened by being involved in serious decision making, they were able and keen to participate as well as being good at it. However, to make choices regarding care and treatment, they needed to be informed.

Hinds' research also found that young people questioned were particularly concerned for others. These adolescents who had been ill for a time were making decisions about undergoing experimental treatment in a bid to help others.

Support groups are an excellent way for the child with a chronic illness to interact with peers. Through a support group, the child can meet in a safe environment with children experiencing the same issues as themselves.

Children who are chronically ill are more vulnerable to depression. Children in this age group are old enough to understand the long-term implications of their illness or condition, and can feel overwhelmed by the demands of treatment. If the parent is concerned that they are depressed, they should talk to the medical team and ask to be referred to a clinical psychologist.

Body image at this age becomes an issue and changes in the appearance due to the illness or treatment can be difficult to accept. Building and enhancing self-esteem is of paramount importance for this group. Children who spend long periods of time in hospital or out of school should be encouraged to develop a hobby or occupation that they can excel at. If possible, they should be given online access to email their friends and keep up to date with their school work. This reinforces their self-worth and helps to compensate for the sense of missing out. Friendships are important and if at all possible should be encouraged and nurtured. School friends should be encouraged to visit.

Education at this stage is important and if possible the child should be encouraged to keep up with their studies. The school should be supportive and assign a teacher to visit the hospital and prepare appropriate work.

It is important to provide the child with opportunities to discuss their feelings. Sometimes children in this age group are reluctant to talk openly to parents. If this is the case, try to identify a person within the family, a teacher, a youth worker or one of the medical team whom the child can talk to.

Specialist teenage units enable young people to have treatment within a hospital environment that has been created for their needs. It is demoralizing for a teenager to be treated on a paediatric ward. Young people need to be able to talk to other young people experiencing the same problems. They can support each other.

The demands of treatment and dealing with repeated or lengthy hospital stays affect the whole family. The most beneficial coping strategy to employ during hospitalization and treatment is to adhere to treatment and be committed to the healthcare plan, adapting to the changes caused by the condition and being proactive in seeking information and addressing problems and challenges as they arise.

❖ Advice and action points ❖

- *Acknowledge* each other's worries and concerns about treatment, and discuss with your medical team how to address them.

- *Learn* how the treatment will affect your child. What are the side-effects of the drugs? How can you lessen their impact? Take notes to enable you to build up a picture of how treatments will affect your child.

- *Expect* your child to be treated with dignity and respect, and complain if you feel this is not happening.

- *Identify* how your child can have a say in treatment and medical procedures: choices help the child to feel in control.

- *Practise* pain-relieving techniques – for example, controlled breathing, guided imagery and visualization techniques – at home before you need to implement them.

- *Care* for yourself and your partner; do not allow yourself to become over-tired or run down. Ask for time out when you can. Talk to other parents on the ward; often they are a source of support and comfort as well as of shared information. Talking about frustrations or worries helps to lessen them or put them into perspective.

- *Foster* a climate of trust to facilitate interdependence between your family and the medical team. The family and the medics need to work together to serve each other's interests.

- *Engage in* face-to-face interaction, which enables a relationship to develop; when possible, have a meeting with the medics rather than relying on telephone consultations or using GPs as intermediaries.

- *Research* treatment options; ask your medical team for direction on where to access information. Ask for second opinions if you are in doubt.

- *Identify* key hospital personnel, outside the immediate clinical medical team, who can help – for example, play therapists, psychologists, social workers, child life specialists, occupational therapists, music therapists.

- *Inform* your child of the benefits and side-effects of treatment, and give them choices when possible.

- *Plan* for hospital stays and procedures. Be informed of risks and how to respond to emergency situations. Have an overnight bag packed for emergencies. Being organized at home will alleviate the stress when staying in hospital.

- *Encourage* hobbies, interests and activities that can be carried out in a hospital environment to pass the time – for example, model making, craft work, reading, writing journals, computer gaming.

- *Support* friendships on the hospital ward and encourage friends from school to visit.

- *Discuss*, within the family, ways in which to make hospital stays easier. Encourage siblings to visit. Be honest and open with your child in age-appropriate terms. Acknowledge their fears and worries, while offering affirmative action in the form of treatment.

- *Bring* comforting items from home – for example, pillows, comforters, special toys. For long-term stays, create a home away from home. Work with the medics to create a care plan that is flexible and family friendly.

- *Ask* for help from family and friends during periods of treatment and hospital stays. Delegate school runs and household chores. Remember to eat and rest when in hospital and to take care of yourself. It is sometimes difficult for parents to eat well in hospital, relying on sandwiches and snacks in the absence of home-cooked meals. Try to access the hospital canteen or ask family to bring home-cooked meals to you.

- *Keep* family and friends informed throughout hospital stays – identify one key person to cascade information in order to reduce the need to contact several people. Expect a period of adjustment both when going into hospital and returning home.

You now understand something of your child's treatment and have explored ways in which you can ease the strain of hospital stays. Working with the medical team and practitioners more widely, you are now doing something positive to help your child with a chronic illness.

3

Communication:
A Two-way Street

Communication affects all areas of our lives. Relationships are constructed and conducted through effective communication. How a diagnosis of chronic illness is communicated can have long-term effects on how a family copes. Evidence shows that anger and resentment caused by a badly handled diagnosis can have a detrimental effect on the doctor and parents' future relationship.

Communication is a two-way street. While patients and parents of patients are often critical of poor communication in hospitals, medics are also dependent on understanding symptoms and problems as communicated to them. The parent and the medic each have a responsibility to the child to work together to deliver the best healthcare possible. Effective communication is essential to achieve the optimal care. In gathering and disseminating knowledge, medics are responding to the parents' need for inclusion. Parents cannot fully commit to the child's treatment unless they have an understanding of what is involved both in the immediate period and in the future. Medics who actively work to help parents become knowledgeable about the child's condition are implementing family-centred care.

Family and friends often say the wrong things even when they have the best intentions. People are not comfortable with illness and even less so when it is a child who is affected. Chronic illness can be frightening. People fear the effects of the illness on the parents and, rather than say the wrong thing, some people say nothing at all. Family and friends should take their lead from the parents when it comes to talking to the child with a chronic illness. If those close to the child know more about their illness and long-term consequences than the child, there is a risk that they will overhear in general conversations more than the parent wants them to know.

Explaining the illness and the impact of the treatment to outsiders is sometimes difficult. One single parent found that she couldn't communicate to those around her how she felt and, as a result, she had less support: 'I sometimes think I appeared to cope too well. People thought I just got up and got on with it but inside I was being torn apart. I was completely empty, gutted from the inside out.' Her inability to explain how she was feeling and how difficult it was to cope with her child's hospitalizations and treatment led to her feeling isolated. Those close to her thought she was coping well and were not aware that she needed practical help and emotional support.

Sometimes relationships go wrong and communication breaks down. Caring for a child with a chronic illness is a stressful and often lengthy process, and over a period of time the parent may encounter individual medics who for one reason or another they do not like. They may not always agree with the medic's decisions or like their approach. The relationship with the medical team may be good but a decision over treatment may be questioned and disagreements can arise. Chronic illness is often for life, and it is impossible to experience long-term healthcare without encountering some area of divergence. When the relationship between the doctor and the parents is good and has followed a pattern of shared collaboration and understanding, then differences will be more readily resolved. Each party needs to explain their concerns and fully explore options available.

If a resolution cannot be reached and the relationship with the medical team or one individual professional is particularly strained, then the parents should put their concerns in writing. Anger and distress can make communication difficult and in the heat of the moment we can make rash judgements and decisions. By writing out our concerns and worries, we can gain clarity of thought and are more likely to offer reasonable arguments to support our viewpoint. Sometimes it is worth copying a letter to someone else in the medical team or the hospital management to ensure a follow-up course of action.

Changes in staff personnel or the introduction of a new phase of treatment may mean that the child is in the care of a new set of people and the process of learning to work together begins all over again. When a child is moving on within the health system or a new medic is introduced, it is important that information is shared so that the child continues to receive the same care. Continuity can be achieved if communication is ongoing and effective and information is disseminated.

With the introduction of multimedia communication systems in hospitals, we will soon be able to contact family and friends online via high-speed internet access. Some hospitals are piloting websites where patients can leave messages and updates on their progress for family and friends to access. Soon we should also be able to access our test results from home online. The wider use of technology in hospitals should improve communication, and make access to patient information quicker and easier. For the thousands of children with a chronic illness confined to hospital wards every year, computer technology is providing a means of communication that offers an opportunity to enhance their self-esteem, help them tolerate treatment and advance their recovery.

Research carried out by Professor Jane Grimson and Paula Hicks of the Centre for Health Informatics, Department of Computer Science, Trinity College Dublin, and colleagues in the Children's Research Centre, Trinity College Dublin, has led to the creation of an online community that connects previously isolated children to their friends and family.

The two closely related projects, Áit Eile (Another World) and Solas, have established a virtual community for children that are chronically ill with the objective of connecting them to the outside world and enhancing their psychological wellbeing.

Áit Eile first began six years ago while Solas has been a more recent undertaking aimed at more isolated children who have perhaps had bone marrow transplants or are receiving treatment for severe burns and are at risk of infection. Professor Grimson described the outcome of the projects:

> We have established a virtual community for children with a
> chronic illness with the objective of reducing their sense of

isolation. They were provided with the means to email, MSN texting, video conferencing with school mates and potentially with their families.

The idea was to reduce the sense of isolation of children with a chronic illness through distraction and communication. We have achieved those objectives and improved their psychological wellbeing.

These children can be in isolation for long periods of time and can be less well at certain periods so they had unsupervised use of their own laptop. The nursing staff have a very close connection with the children and they have been very positive.

We are now looking at other target groups such as dialysis patients who spend several hours, three to four days a week, connected to a machine.

While Professor Grimson does not claim that the children's recovery is directly improved by the computer access, she does believe the psychosocial benefits enhance the child's ability to cope with their condition: 'The psychological benefits are clear and the children tolerate treatment a little better.'

A further benefit of the programme was to provide children with a continuity of support from health professionals. As Professor Grimson explained:

We also found one side benefit for children with brain injuries who have to be transferred for rehabilitation to somewhere else, are able to be introduced to staff with video conferencing and when they move to a new place they can chat back to the old staff.

Effective use of technology in the healthcare system can enhance levels of communication. Medics will have greater access to medical records, better co-ordination of test results and a more efficient transfer of information to the patient.

Medics need to provide parents with a vast array of information when a child is diagnosed with a chronic condition: clinical information regarding the child's symptoms and condition, information on their treatment and possible side-effects, along with information on more practical matters such as how care plans will be implemented.

The clinical information is derived from the medical team, research and through talking to other people who have experience of the same condition. More practical information relates to the details concerning the hospital – how far is it from the family home? Is parking convenient? What are meal times and visiting times? Can siblings spend time on the ward? What are the ward facilities? Can parents shower on the ward? Should parents change bed sheets or carry out laundry? Can they have access to the medical notes while on the ward? Information regarding practical details is needed to enable the family to cope with the day-to-day living during hospital stays.

Parents also need information regarding the child's education. Often the voluntary organizations and charities connected to the child's condition can provide practical information of this kind.

Communicating with health professionals

For years doctors have had a reputation for being poor communicators. So-called 'bedside manner' is dependent on the personality of the individual coupled with training and experience. However, good communication is more than a slick bedside manner. Being perceived as nice and friendly helps but simply isn't enough.

Thankfully good communication can be taught to an extent. Medicine is not about the research of lofty ideas and hypotheses studied and tested in laboratories; instead, it is about patients first and foremost. Most doctors have gone into the field of medicine because they want to help people – it is a people-centred occupation.

The majority of medics now receive training in communication. Doctors are required on an almost daily basis to explain often complex information in terms understandable to the lay person. Doing this under pressure, in demanding situations when devastating news has to be given to parents, is one of the most demanding aspects of being a doctor.

I can remember hearing a story about an eminent physician lecturing to a large group of medical students about diabetes. The physician began telling them about the patient's family; the patient was married to a baker's daughter and lived next door to the alehouse. He would come home from work and eat dinner and then pick up a parcel of left-over cakes from his father-in-law before heading off for a drink with his friends at the alehouse.

At the end of the lecture, the physician concluded that the patient was a diabetic. One very irate student stood up and said: 'We have learnt nothing about diabetes. This has been a waste of time,' to which the physician replied: 'Ah indeed, but you have learnt much about your patient and his lifestyle and family background which are all contributory factors to his wellbeing.'

The student had fallen for the physician's trap. Any medical text book could tell them the science of diabetes, or enzymes and glucose levels, but the physician had taught the students a valuable lesson – understanding the patient is as important as understanding the disease.

Doctors need to have a broad range of communication ability, being able to interact and communicate medical information to a variety of people with different abilities and backgrounds. The medic's role in relation to the parent is to assist and support them in their care for their child. Through good communication, the doctor is able to empower the parent with knowledge that will help them understand their child's condition and deliver care and treatment according to the doctor's instructions.

In *Counselling Parents of Children with Chronic Illness or Disability*, Hilton Davis states: 'Ideally, if they [parents] construe professionals as helpful, understanding, trustworthy, supportive and respectful, then the parents' ability to cope with the disease and treatment is likely to be enhanced, or at least not hindered.'[1]

The parents' ability to cope can be influenced by their relationship with the doctors and nursing staff. If the parents feel supported and involved in their child's treatment, then they are more likely to adapt to the diagnosis and cope with long-term care. Their relationship with the medical team can be determined by good communication.

Unfortunately most doctors view communication with patients to be about clinical diagnosis. They seek information on symptoms and respond by giving information on medication. Good communication is about creating and fostering relationships, much more than the imparting of clinical information. Often a patient's emotional wellbeing will have an effect on their physical wellbeing. A good doctor will recognize the need to be familiar with their patient, to *know* them. Medics need to assess the child's background to have an awareness of the infrastructure and to gauge the coping ability of the family. They must also have awareness of the child's cultural or religious background and show respect for their traditions. In order to achieve this, the medic must endeavour to build a relationship with the family.

Parents want the health professionals to listen to their concerns, to be respectful of their role as parents and to acknowledge their expertise where their child is concerned. To create a partnership between the parents and the health professionals that allows for the sharing of information, good communication is essential.

The diagnosis consultation is perhaps the most difficult. The doctor is required to inform parents of bad news and explain often complex information. While there may be treatment options and hope of management of the condition, ultimately a diagnosis of chronic illness will be distressing. Health professionals should give realistic outcomes, detailing treatment options and citing contingencies as to why certain courses of action may not work. Outlining the hardships and long-term demands of a chronic condition can seem demoralizing but, if the difficulties are not dwelt on and are put in context, then the family will be grateful for the realism. Parents want to be reassured that their child is going to receive the best care and treatment available. How a doctor comes across in a consultation is seen as being representative of the entire hospital. We all make judgements, and how the parents perceive the doctor will determine how they feel about the entire medical establishment.

One of the most common complaints about the diagnosis consultation is that the doctor has informed the parent in a non-sympathetic way. The information has been delivered in a blunt manner, seemingly uncaring. While a doctor may consider their delivery as being straightforward and direct, a parent may consider it to be cold and clinical. How the diagnosis is delivered has a lasting impact on the parents and, inadvertently, on how they cope with their child's condition.

Some parents have been informed in corridors or even on the telephone. While there is no easy way to impart the news that a child has a chronic illness, which in some instances may be life threatening, most health professionals would acknowledge that empathy and understanding are necessary.

The doctor informing the parents of the diagnosis should pay close attention to their reactions. If they are openly distressed, it is worth allowing them a moment to compose themselves before continuing the consultation slowly and gently. The parents may need to be comforted and reassured before they can continue to listen to the information. Before the end of the consultation, it is important that the doctor establishes what the parents understand: have they interpreted the information correctly and do they have any questions?

Above all, the doctor must ensure that the parents have a good, clear understanding of the diagnosis and some idea of the prognosis. If treatment is an option, they should be provided with a follow-up appointment to discuss the next stage. The shock of the diagnosis disclosure can prevent some parents from absorbing the full impact of the news. As one mother described her experience, 'It took a while for reality to set in. Even though I had been told what was wrong with my child, I didn't really understand.'

Research has shown that most parents feel they have not been given enough information about the child's condition and long-term implications:

> Physicians regularly underestimated parents' apparently insatiable desire for information about the child's chronic condition(s) and its implications. While parents state their desire for more information consistently and independently of severity and diagnostic categories, paediatricians seem to be more aware of this need for information *among* children with neurologic conditions, and those whose conditions have resulted in greater impact on the family ('intensity'), than *among* other children.[2]

When one mother was informed about her son's diagnosis of leukaemia, she had to wait three days before meeting a relevant consultant:

> I needed to speak to someone straight away to put my mind at ease and answer my questions. I needed to know how serious the illness was and how common. I wanted to know how they would go about treating him but I had to wait.

Many parents will relate to the notion of doctors treating them, especially mothers, as being over-protective and neurotic. Prior to the diagnosis, the parents, and it is usually the mother, will have made repeated visits to the

GP and health visitor, voicing their concerns. This sense of not being listened to or understood can often make parents wary of trusting medics following the diagnosis. The parents will have had their worst fears realized and will be hesitant in accepting that they are being taken seriously. Doctors need to understand that the parent's concern can be helpful in alerting them to problems with the child.

Not so many years ago, it was unlikely for a parent to question a doctor or to disagree with their advice. Doctors worked in isolation from the parents and issued instructions, cascading information from the top down. Now much of the healthcare for the child with a chronic illness is administered at home. The doctors have to work in partnership with the parents and good communication is required to ensure the child is receiving the best treatment. It is necessary for health professionals to manage the child's care in partnership with their parents. Parents need to feel respected and listened to, and that they are working with the healthcare team rather than being controlled by them.

The balance of power has moved away from the medical profession to the parents. As parents have become more active in the healthcare of children, medics have been forced to improve their communication skills. Parents are more inclined to research their child's condition and challenge the medical profession when they are not satisfied.

The relationship between the doctor and the parent forms an intricate part of the child's treatment. There exists interdependence between the parents and the medics – each needs the other to fulfil their role in caring for the child. Good communication ensures that this relationship is effective.

When the child is an adolescent, the doctor–patient relationship becomes more complex – at what stage does the young person have the right to be in control of information relating to their condition and healthcare? The confidentiality of the young person needs to be respected with doctors balancing the needs of the patient with those of their parents. Parents must be respectful of the young person's need for information and privacy. The young person may choose to attend hospital appointments without their parents or wish to make decisions regarding their treatment which do not correspond to their parents' wishes. It is through ongoing good communication between the medical team, the parents and the young person that differences can be addressed and resolved.

Communication between the doctor and the parent is an important factor in determining the coping ability of the family. Doctors are limited in recognizing the needs of the child if they do not interact and communicate with the family. A medic cannot prescribe treatment and make judgements about the child's wellbeing if they do not form a relationship with the family. To create a relationship, there must be regular communication. The identification of the needs of the child and the family contributes to the parents' sense of being listened to and cared for. Without actively trying to ascertain and understand the family's needs, the healthcare team cannot respond to and address these needs.

Parents need to feel that their child's medical team cares.[3] Some people are naturally compassionate and can relate their feelings with ease. Others convey information in a cold, aloof or clinical way. They may be no less feeling, but they cannot convey their emotions in a work environment. Non-verbal communication can compensate for a more non-expressive personality. Taking someone's hand or giving them a hug can say more than a long rambling speech. For the medic to support the family in emotional terms, they need to have a caring approach. If the parents feel that the medic is compassionate and sensitive to their feelings, then their distress will be minimized. While there is no perfect way to deliver bad news, the parents' trauma can be lessened if the medic is able to disclose information in a compassionate manner. The diagnosis disclosure is not the only instance of such a delivery. Often chronic illness will unfold and change as the child grows and develops. The condition may worsen with progression and tests and further disclosures will be necessary.

Above all, the parent wants to see the medic communicate well with their child. Old-fashioned attitudes to titles can alienate children and young people from their medical team. In *Hannah's Gift: Lessons from a Life Fully Lived*, Maria Housden recounts how her two-year-old daughter stopped a medical examination because she felt uneasy with so many people in the room whom she sensed were not her friends because they had not introduced themselves. Housden realized that Hannah deserved respect and supported her daughter's demand to know the doctor's name. When he responded 'Dr Fiorelli', Hannah said, 'No, your *real* name.'[4]

A first-name basis will create a sense of ease and familiarity. By the same token, children do not respond well to white coats. Most paediatric wards have relaxed dress codes, which communicates a sense of friendliness to the patients. Children and young people respond to expressiveness and eye contact. They do not want to be 'talked over', patronized or belittled. They deserve respect.

Listening is as important as speaking in communicating. Doctors who face malpractice suits are often perceived as poor communicators who have often been unavailable to their patients. Listening requires patience and quiet. It is often difficult for doctors to have an uninterrupted consultation with a patient – beepers go off, other staff members have queries, and so on. A designated room for consultations would help. Doctors need to make time and, if the parents feel that they have issues that still need to be addressed, they can suggest scheduling a further appointment.

Doctors are often guilty of taking notes while listening. While note-taking is important, it is also vital to read a person's mannerisms and expressions. Eye contact reassures the patient or the parent that the doctor is listening rather than just looking for diagnostic clues. Active listening means that a doctor is listening and watching while responding to the patient's body language and mannerisms. Through eye contact we are responding to a person rather than just listening to their words. Of course, work load and time constraints dictate that the doctor is often unable to provide the patient or the parent with uninterrupted quality listening time.

A doctor who is willing to listen, understand a patient's concerns, respond in a caring fashion and make time for meaningful consultations is less likely to be sued for malpractice. Research indicates that, if patients feel that their concerns are listened to, they are less likely to attribute blame when things go wrong.

For parents to feel valued by the medical profession and to be active decision makers in their child's treatment, a relationship of openness and trust needs to be fostered. In exchanging information and communicating effectively, the doctor–patient relationship is strengthened and the medic can have a fuller appreciation of the concerns affecting the patient while the patient or parent can be better informed about the condition and treatment.

Communication is a two-way exchange: we speak to express our views and we listen to understand. Our assessment of a doctor's abilities is not based on league tables and statistics. Instead we rely on our instinct – do we click? Do we feel comfortable and safe with them? These judgements are made from how they come across through communication. A patient's or a parent's satisfaction is dependent on their relationship with their doctor. A good patient–doctor relationship can also influence wellbeing and success of treatment. To treat a patient, the doctor needs to understand their background, to have knowledge of their living situation, their home life and their relationships. Having an interest in someone as a person rather than an unusual medical case is important.

The child's needs are often interpreted differently by doctors compared to parents. Communication helps medics to understand the child's needs and those of the family; this is essential when services are being developed. Young people are often able to identify and voice their needs better than their parents, and then should be consulted by the medics and support services.

When the patient and family are consulted on an ongoing basis, they are more likely to feel satisfied and cared for by the healthcare system. Parents appreciate having their input recognized by medics and feel valued when their opinion is called upon. This sense of worth helps the parents to cope and enhances their self-esteem. When the parents and the medics work together, highlighting needs and discrepancies in perceived needs, they can create a more complete family-centred care plan. Regular and ongoing communication is the means to achieving this.

Research carried out to assess the agreement among fathers, mothers and paediatricians about the unmet needs of children with chronic health conditions found that doctors seemed to under-estimate the need that parents felt for information regarding the day-to-day management of their child's condition, mothers' need for help in facilitating social contact, and both parents' need for help in co-ordinating their child's overall health and developmental circumstances.[5]

The doctor–patient dialogue needs to be two-way. When the patient is a child, this communication becomes triplicate. To treat the child, the doctor must also be considerate of the parents. Even enlightened doctors, who acknowledge the need for family-centred care and recognize the difficulties in caring for children that are chronically ill, cannot realize the full extent of the family's needs unless there exists a mechanism for dialogue. Doctors are sometimes called upon to speak at support groups but actually more could be achieved if they listened to parents speaking at such groups. Engaging with parents outside the clinical hospital setting is one way of exploring families' needs and developing effective communication.

If the wellbeing and concerns of the parents are overlooked, then the medics are failing the child. A parent who is not coping cannot adequately care for a child with a chronic illness. The diagnosis disclosure can be an indicator of how well a parent will cope.

Often doctors are not aware of the life-changing nature of a chronic disease. They see the child and the immediate impact of the symptoms, but they need to view the whole picture: the implications for the family dynamic, the long-term worries, and the emotional and financial costs of living with chronic illness. In seeing the whole picture, the doctor will be better able to treat the child fully and assist the family in the process of living with chronic illness.

Parents need communication to be pitched at their level without their being patronized or spoken to in medical jargon. Information should be presented in straightforward language with medical terminology explained if necessary. Parents want to feel that their child's medical team care, and it is through good communication that a doctor can convey empathy. Often a relaxed chat and a smile can do wonders in enhancing the patient–doctor relationship.

Consultation appointments are most effective if the parent is able to communicate their concerns. The triplicate nature of the parent–child–doctor relationship dictates that sometimes communication can be difficult. The parent is often speaking on behalf of the child. The parent and the child should prepare a shortlist before consultations to ensure their time is used most effectively. The most important issue should be raised first. The doctor relies on the parents to communicate the child's problems to them and to explain any developments or changes since the previous appointment. At clinic appointments, any pending test results should be disclosed and noted and a follow-up appointment made.

Parents need to understand how test results are communicated. Do they wait for following appointments to be told blood results or can they telephone to be updated? Can they contact the radiology department direct for scan results, or is there a protocol dictating that the child's consultant should relay the information? Sometimes it is necessary to challenge how test results are communicated. If one hospital department is waiting for another to communicate results to them before informing the parent, then time can be wasted unnecessarily. Parents should be able to raise these issues with the medics in order to find ways to improve the flow of information.

Test results are meaningless without knowledge. The parent needs to ask the medical team to explain the results. Nurses are often the best people to ask for this type of information. The parents should ask for a reference as to what a normal result should be, and what a result likely to cause concern would be.

Some doctors believe that parents do not need to be given detailed test results, preferring instead to give a broad indication. I feel that the parent should demand to know. There is a safeguard in parents questioning test results. On one occasion when Owen was scheduled to have chemotherapy, he had a blood test taken in the morning with the chemo due to begin following hydration at night. When we arrived on the ward, I asked for his blood results and the nurse said he would get them for me when he had a chance. It was a busy ward and I asked a further two times. On the third occasion, I was told the blood results must have been fine because the chemo had been ordered from the pharmacy by the day time nursing staff. I accepted this and settled down for the night with Owen, knowing his chemo pump would begin some time during the night.

At 3 am, the same nurse woke me to say he had checked the blood results and Owen's platelets were dangerously low. The chemo had to be stopped in order to administer an immediate platelet transfusion. The nurse, a very competent, caring man, was apologetic. It was a lesson for both of us – he, it was hoped, would not make assumptions again and I wouldn't be fobbed off with 'the results must have been fine'.

Communicating with parents

Parents are often required to recount the 'story' of their child's illness to medics, family and friends. Through talking about the diagnosis, we begin to process the information and gradually begin to accept the situation. We describe the physical ramifications, the emotional journey, the sense of loss, anger, frustrations, and the highs and lows.

I have often been asked about the presentation of Owen's brain tumour. People have asked me how his tumour was diagnosed. I have lost count of the number of times I have told people about the week leading up to Owen's diagnosis at the age of two.

I have described how on the Monday morning he was reluctant to get out of bed. We had to take his sister, Kate, to school: a short ten-minute walk, which we undertook every weekday with Owen in his pushchair. But every time I managed to take Owen out of bed and dress him, he would try to crawl back up the stairs.

He seemed tired and lethargic and out of sorts but, by mid-morning, he was able to go to a play session with me. By Wednesday he had not improved so I took him to see the GP. He lay like a baby in my arms as the GP gave him a thorough examination. I could not give her specific symptoms, just a vague sense that something was wrong. I told her I felt he wasn't thriving. He was such a good child, almost too good.

Developmentally he was on target so I had no reason to suspect a brain tumour. My understanding of a brain tumour was that it would present with disability. But here was my two-year-old son showing symptoms of nothing worse than a virus. Significantly though, when the GP asked had Owen run a fever, I said no. A sick child without a fever is not always a cause for concern, but it should have alerted the GP that there was something more sinister going on. The GP was satisfied that Owen was well enough to go home. I had asked for a further referral to see a consultant paediatrician. Owen had been referred to a paediatrician when he was just over a year old but they had found no problems. The GP didn't think it was necessary and asked why; my answer was simply 'because he is too good'. He wasn't climbing or playing with the same robustness as other two-year-olds. I couldn't explain my deepest fear that Owen wasn't going to be with me forever. The GP's reply was to come back in a couple of weeks if I was still concerned.

By the Friday morning, Owen seemed to have improved and we visited my friends Zoe and Paul. While at Zoe and Paul's house, Owen began to walk unsteadily and hold his head to the side. Zoe assumed it was an ear infection and called the GP's surgery for me to get an appointment for after lunch.

Owen and I went home and I phoned my mum. Her advice was to just go to the hospital. My neighbour was a nurse so I rang her. She didn't give me an option – within minutes she was at my front door with the car running. We rushed off with Owen's comforter, my old satin nightie, and his bottle in case it was a long haul. It was three weeks before we were home again and in that time everything in our lives had changed beyond recognition.

At the hospital Owen co-operated with all the neurological tests, bemused to be entertained by a variety of medics. He didn't seem to be in any pain or discomfort unless walking, but every so often he would say, 'Mum mum, hug.' He would fold into me and we would snuggle together, his soft curly blond hair just below my chin. I was asked about his medical history several times – he had had a long birth, was breastfed until 11 months, was hospitalized with breathing difficulties at four weeks; from a year old, he had a pattern of repeated viruses and he was reluctant to try new foods. I had taken him to the GP frequently and at around 16 months he had seen a hospital paediatrician who had tested him for every illness from coeliac disease, which I have, to liver function and thyroid problems.

There was no reason to look for something neurological. He was a bright, affectionate child who had reached all his milestones on target.

I phoned my husband, Liam, at work and told him to meet me at the hospital. I explained that so far all I had been told by a registrar was that there could be something seriously wrong with Owen's brain. Despite all our worrying, this seemed far-fetched.

Although Liam and I worried about him constantly, it was born out of a sense of unease rather than particular symptoms. Later that night, Owen was sedated to enable a CT scan to be undertaken. We watched as he was laid out on a trolley, still and deathly pale, dressed in a hospital gown, waiting for the scanner to rotate around him. It was a foreboding image, which stayed with us throughout the years.

We were told the devastating news, around 9 pm on that Friday night in a room separate from our sleeping son. There were around five medics seated facing us while the consultant explained slowly and quietly what they had discovered. The scan revealed a mass at the back of Owen's head. We were so distraught that the consultant had to stop every now and again to allow us to regain some composure before he went on. He was visibly affected and I have always felt immense gratitude that he seemed to really care about us and, more importantly, about Owen.

In an instant everything was altered. The life we thought we had designed for ourselves disintegrated on that Friday night.

In retelling the story of Owen's diagnosis, I have been looking for clues. Could I have done something sooner or different? Recounting stories is in itself a form of therapy. We also relate our experiences to others in order to reinforce memories and to make sense of events.

At the point of being told the diagnosis of a chronic condition, all parents experience a variety of emotions from feeling shock to a sense of bereavement. The news is devastating and has a lasting impact. Many parents speak of how traumatized they were at receiving the news, and how they always remember that day.[6]

Often families have more than one diagnosis day – children can be symptom-free for a period of time before becoming ill again, and the breaking of bad news may have to be relived. Sometimes further complications arise and the full extent of the diagnosis unfolds over time. The impact of the diagnosis and, significantly, *how it is communicated* to parents is of great importance. How a diagnosis is imparted can have ramifications for the future relationship between the family and the medical profession. The diagnosis consultation can cause lasting damage to the relationship or it can at best help prepare the way for a good partnership between the medics and the parents.

To deliver a diagnosis is difficult. Medics do not like giving bad news, especially when it concerns a child. There are ways to communicate the information without causing further distress than necessary to the parents. Parents should be told the information together, in a private room, if possible without the child being present. Single parents should be asked if they would like a relative or friend with them – the shock of a diagnosis often renders the information meaningless, and having a second person present helps to piece together what has been said.

More than one health professional should be present; often a nurse or social worker can sit in on a consultation to help the parents clarify the information. It is better if the diagnosis is delivered by someone who has treated the child and knows the parents. The language used should be clear and concise. Parents find it difficult to absorb information when it has come as a shock. They will ask questions and seek further information. Options and choices can be explained, but parents should not be required to make decisions at the diagnosis stage unless it is absolutely vital to the health of the child.

Communicating with your child

Living with chronic illness has an impact on all areas of a child's life: their home life is affected, their school life and their social network. This creates different communicative needs: the child or young person needs to understand how their illness affects them physically, and how it can have an impact on them psychologically. Through the communication of the dual impact of the condition, the physical and the emotional, the child or young person is better equipped to deal with the physical problems and the social or psychological issues.[7]

Children and young people need to have a basic understanding of biology, how their treatments are effective and how they can work with medical staff to improve their wellbeing. Psychological needs relate to an understanding of how their emotions can be altered by the limitations of their condition, how their medications can cause side-effects altering their emotions and how they can cope with the emotional burden of living with a chronic condition. Children and young people living with chronic illness can experience negative feelings relating to their body image and their sense of who they are. Being able to recognize and communicate these emotions can help their adjustment and coping ability, and even prevent the onset of depression.

While all children and young people need to have information relating to their condition, it is not appropriate to deliver the same level of information to all. Each child will have different needs and varying levels of understanding, and communication of their condition has to be tailored to meet their needs. As the child grows and develops, so too will their need for information. Chronic illness is often a changing and fluctuating condition and the levels of communication need to be adapted accordingly.

The language of illness can be negative and it is a challenge for parents to communicate with their child about their condition without using language which suggests negativity. How a parent speaks about tests can affect the child's morale. 'He got a bad result' suggests that the child is in some way responsible for the outcome of the medical test and has therefore failed the parents. Similarly, speaking of the need to fight the illness suggests a level of responsibility to combat the condition on the child's part. For this reason, I dislike the term 'survivor' because it implies that those who have not survived have in some way not been strong enough.

When communicating to a child about illness and treatment, the language used needs to be age appropriate. Terms such as 'shot' for injection is more visual and threatening; an X-ray or scan can be intimidating unless it is seen as a mere photographic tool. Think in the child's terms – simplify. A blood test is often about counting red cells and white cells; investigative surgery is about having a look inside the body, not being cut open. 'IV', or 'intravenous', means that something is administered directly into a vein. Access to the veins in many children with a chronic illness is through a port or central line. This line, known as the Hickman Line but often referred to as Mr Wiggly on paediatric wards, is to enable frequent IV treatments, either chemo, transfusions or antibiotics. When the medical equipment and procedures are described in non-threatening language, the child will be less frightened.

Every health condition has its own language or jargon. The child diagnosed with diabetes will learn about insulin, ketones, blood sugars, highs and lows, hypos, etc. This new vocabulary can be intimidating and give rise to misunderstandings. Parents can speak about a 'bad blood sugar reading', which can suggest on some level that the child has done something wrong. While control of the child's diet is important for the management of diabetes, a teenager may feel restricted by the sense of being controlled, and rebel through non-compliance with treatment. Children with coeliac disease are required to follow a gluten-free diet, which is often described by parents as a 'special diet'; again, the implication is that the child is in some way labelled, restricted and controlled.

There has been much research and discussion about the child's 'right to know'. To deny a child information pertaining to their health and treatment is isolating and damaging. To cope with their condition, they need to have a good understanding of their illness and to be able to communicate how they feel to others. They can participate in discussions with their medics and be part of the decision-making process if they have been included in the information process with their parents and have fostered a relationship of openness and trust.

Many parents find that they are selective about the information they tell the child, even an adolescent.[8] Information becomes managed and censored.[9]

To some extent we are all guilty of this: we do not want to voice our fears to our children, to alarm them about their illness. Parents seek to portray themselves to their children as in control and optimistic about the outcome. While parents are trying to protect the child, they are also denying them full involvement. As Dr Anthony McCarthy has found, the trust between a child and their parents can be compromised if they do not share information about the diagnosis:

> These children, at some stage, will find out either through other patients or parents on the ward or in fact other medical or nursing staff members. If they haven't been told by their parents they will certainly lose trust in these carers in a time when they are most needed. As a medical professional my advice would be to answer a direct question honestly and explain things as carefully as possible to the child so they can understand.

Children are not easily duped. Omitting information can in itself cause them distress when they sense that the parent is not being honest. A reluctance to discuss chronic illness and the possibility of death isolates the child and leaves them to deal with their fears alone.

One parent found that, although she never had a proper full discussion with her son about his leukaemia, he gradually gained an awareness and understanding of his illness: 'He had to grow up a lot quicker. He knew what was going on and that he had sick blood. I told him about his medicine and that he had to stay in hospital to get better.'

A study conducted by Dr Bryony Beresford, research fellow at the University of York, highlighted the wide-ranging information needs of children and young people. These needs were categorized into either medical or psychosocial information needs.[10] Psychosocial information needs are derived from the need to manage the impact of the condition on the emotional, social and educational aspects of a young person's life as well as their future prospects. The young people involved in the study identified these needs as being as important to them as the need for medical information.

Communication about childhood cancer has changed considerably over the last few decades. Informing children and young people of a cancer diagnosis would have been unheard of previously, mainly because many children diagnosed with cancer died. The implication was that to protect the child from knowing how serious their condition was, the parent would withhold information. The benefits of being open and honest, and explaining cancer and its treatment, are now recognized.[11]

Likewise, cystic fibrosis is an incurable condition and, while ten years ago the life expectancy of a child diagnosed with it was an average of 18 years, that average has now been extended to more than 33 years. Discussing such serious conditions with children is difficult and often parents need to have guidance from health professionals.

Communication within the family can change following the diagnosis of a chronic condition.[12] Good communication between the parent and the child is essential for the management of certain conditions. For instance, young people with type 1 diabetes need to be trusted to adhere to treatment and carry out glycaemic control. It is all too easy for parents and adolescents to clash over the management of diabetes. The young person has to be allowed to manage their condition with parental involvement. To prevent conflict, the parents must be able to communicate with the young person about their condition without being judgemental and suspicious.

The child with a chronic illness will ask many questions about their condition. They need basic medical information relating to their condition, investigations and treatments; how their body is affected; how they can manage their condition; and the role of the hospital and the medical professionals in their life. Their psychological information needs relate to relationships with parents, siblings and peers; managing school and social situations; living with uncertainty; and issues of body image and negative emotions. On a basic level they want to know:

- Why am I different?
- Why do I have to go to hospital?
- Why do I have to take medicine?

Often my son, Owen, would ask, 'What do I have to do to get better?' This simple question would break my heart because he was doing everything in his power to comply with treatment. From a very young age, he asked questions about his illness and treatment. He used words like 'neutropenic' with understanding. He knew why he had a portacath fitted and why he needed regular blood and platelet transfusions.

He was aware of his scar, situated at the back of his head, and could explain to peers when he was asked how he got it. He knew why his hair had fallen out and that it would grow back when his chemotherapy ended. He also understood and accepted to a large degree why he had to avoid other children when not on the hospital ward for fear of infection when his white cell count was low. All this was a great deal of information for a young child to understand. Medical language and terminology can be intimidating and frightening. Through understanding and acquiring knowledge, the fear is dispelled.

In spite of Owen being well informed about his brain tumour and treatment, I was horrified to discover that, when he had MRI scans, for which he was given a general anaesthetic, he thought the doctor could see what was going on by taking his head off! We talked to Owen about all aspects of his hospital attendance, but this misunderstanding had escaped us until he was old enough to question it.

Parents and medics need to predict the level at which to direct information. Some children may require detailed descriptions while others, because of age or developmental ability, cannot absorb too much detail.

It is better to talk to a child in a comfortable, familiar environment. If the parent can talk to the child at home in a calm and relaxed manner, the child is more likely to feel at ease in asking questions. It is worth asking the child at intervals to explain what they know about their illness or treatment so that the parent can judge their level of understanding. By questioning the child about their illness, the parent can discover misconceptions and rectify any misunderstandings. Informing the child or young person about aspects of their condition does not have to be a formal sit-down scenario. Instead, the parent can introduce the topic in the car, at meal times, or play time – whenever and wherever the parent and child can talk uninterrupted.

It is worth relating the child's illness or treatment regimes to their real-life scenarios – for instance, help them understand why they cannot go for a sleepover at a friend's house or why they have a restricted diet. You can also help your child to explain their illness to others. Teasing or bullying born out of ignorance or fear of someone being different can be eliminated through informing and educating. Teachers also need to be informed about the child's condition (see Chapter 5, The Education and Learning Experience).

Children are the primary source of information about their progress; after all, it is how they relate or present their symptoms that directs the medics. I can remember attending a clinic appointment with Owen and telling his doctor that he had been experiencing palpitations. The consultant looked at me as if to ask how I could possibly know. We had a good, relaxed relationship by this stage. He turned to Owen and asked how he felt, to which Owen replied, 'Well, my heart is kind of jumpy.' Enough said!

It is difficult to predict how a child will react to information about their condition. Some children will be accepting while others will display anger and denial. You need to be able to reassure your child that they are not alone; that they are loved and supported by their family. It is useful to encourage them to talk about their feelings. Some children and particularly adolescents try to avoid doing so for fear of upsetting their parents.

Many parents report that their children display remarkable resilience and accept their illness and treatment without complaint. One parent said, 'During the illness he never complained once. He took his medication and did his school work with a tutor without complaining, so what right did I have to complain?'

If you are over-emotional when discussing the illness with your child, then your child may withdraw for fear of causing upset. One of the greatest challenges of caring for a child with a chronic illness is always putting the child's needs first, no matter at what cost emotionally. While you should try to have some control over your emotions when talking to your child, it is all right to cry and share their pain and worries. This teaches them that it is fine to acknowledge that sometimes the illness is upsetting; that we all need to cry at times; and that they will not be judged for showing emotion.

It is worth remembering that a child's information needs will change and develop over the course of their illness; never assume that they understand and ask them periodically if they have any questions. Communication needs to be ongoing and will develop with the child's growth and learning. A child's need for information can be overlooked if they have been born with a condition or diagnosed at a very young age. The parents assume an innate understanding on the part of the child, which may not always be the case. Dr Anthony McCarthy feels that the medic has a responsibility to address the child's concerns: 'More often than not we find that their greatest worries are the easiest things to sort out and it is our job as medical professionals to try and tease out exactly what are their greatest concerns.'

Young people should be given the opportunity to talk directly with their medical team. When Owen was embarking on a course of radiotherapy at the age of five, he heard during a consultation that he would be put on a course of steroids to help control swelling on the brain. Owen had some previous experience of steroids and knew that the side-effects included weight gain particularly around the face. When the consultation ended, he told me that he did not want to have steroids. At a loss as to how to handle Owen's direct response, I asked him if he would like to talk to his consultant about the drugs. Owen and his consultant, who was near retirement age, had become good friends.

Owen explained that he didn't want a big, moon face – a cushingoid appearance being a side-effect of steroids. The consultant explained why the drugs were necessary and with some friendly banter between them he accepted her advice. Hearing the information from the medic had more impact than hearing it from me. They had developed a good relationship through ongoing communication. At every consultation she would speak directly to Owen, enquire how he was feeling, what he had been doing at home and how his school work was progressing. He loved trying to impress her with his reading ability and his knowledge of insects. In taking time to know Owen and to develop a relationship with him, the consultant had ensured that when he was concerned about his treatment she was able to address his worries, and that he trusted her judgement.

Explaining chronic illness to a child is necessary in order to equip them with the understanding to express their symptoms and concerns. The child or young person needs their parents to be honest and open as far as possible. Trust is built on honesty and, if the child feels that they cannot trust their parents, they will be less likely to cope with treatment and procedures.

The child needs to be forewarned about painful procedures and difficult treatment. It can be tempting to tell an anxious child that a procedure will not hurt in order to make them comply and acquiesce but, in doing so, the parent only creates future difficulties for themselves and the child. If the parent lies about the procedure, then trust will be lost.

While many chronic conditions can affect the child physically and lead to poor self-image, the child can only communicate their feelings if they have a good understanding of their illness. Sometimes, especially with younger children, or children with a condition which affects their verbal communication ability, communication through non-verbal means is necessary. Drawing or writing about a condition can help the child express emotions or worries that they find difficulty voicing. Music therapy, art therapy and play therapy are all effective means of tapping into emotions and feelings.

Parents will not always have all the answers to their child's questions. Saying 'I don't know' is an honest admission – and helps the child understand that, while the parent doesn't always have all the answers, they often know who to turn to for advice and information. Throughout the course of chronic illness, the child will inevitably feel that it is unfair that they have to endure limitations and illness. The parent should acknowledge that it is not fair and that it is okay to feel angry. It is only natural to question 'why me?' at times.

Communicating with well siblings

Siblings of children with a chronic illness will cope with the impact on family life if they are fully integrated in the communication of the condition. Resentment and jealousy are common emotions experienced by well siblings. Their lives are disrupted and they can experience difficulties at school and with peers. Siblings will be more understanding and tolerant if they are informed about why the child with a chronic illness requires more attention.[13]

Many siblings, especially those who are young when the diagnosis occurs, feel that they are never properly informed about the condition. One explained, 'The condition wasn't really communicated to me; even now I still don't fully understand. I was young so I grew up with awareness – I just knew his limitations and what eventually was going to happen.'

The parents need to explain more than the physical limitations of the condition. It is important to identify the needs of the well sibling for information. They may not understand the full complexities of the condition and how the child is affected. Their need for information will be ongoing and will change as they develop and grow older. Chronic illness has an ongoing effect on the whole family and the dialogue will be constantly changing. Discussions surrounding medical needs and treatment can be superseded by other life-changing events. Some families move to be closer to specialist treatment centres. Siblings need to understand that such a move is to benefit the siblings as much as the ill child; in helping the child with a chronic illness, the family is better able to cope all round. Moving home can be difficult for the siblings to accept. They may resent the sick child for disrupting their lives. If the family moves to be closer to their extended family, then the siblings can have extra support, especially during long-term hospital stays. Communicating the reasons behind changes helps siblings to be more tolerant and understanding.

Complexities exist for siblings who are potential donors. Siblings are often the best match for bone marrow donations. The donor sibling can experience fear and resentment that they are being put at risk. They often feel they have no choice in the donation and are pressured into responding to the needs of their sick sibling. Support and understanding for the donor sibling is necessary. Concern about hospital procedures and pain can be heightened because of their awareness of their sick sibling's experiences. Counselling and ongoing communication within the family is vital.

How to communicate chronic illness to peers

One of the more challenging aspects of communicating illness is supporting the child or young person in their relationships with their peer group. The child needs to be able to explain their condition, their treatment and how it affects them. Through communication with peers and friends, the young person or child can encourage social inclusion and avoid feeling isolated.

When children are young, they rely on their parents to communicate on their behalf but with the development of adolescence it becomes important for the young person to take responsibility for communicating their condition. They need to develop skills to help them explain why they are limited by their illness, why they need to stay in hospital or attend out-patient appointments and why they require treatment. For a young person to become a good communicator, they need to have active involvement in their care. Through understanding their condition, they can address the questions raised by their peers.

The information needs of a young person will be more advanced than those of a child. However, that is not to say that a child, even a very young child, will have limited needs. They still require clear, open information, which is ongoing and timely. When a young person is included in discussions about their healthcare both at home and in the hospital consultation setting, they will develop the ability to voice their concerns. They need to be recognized as being active in their care, having some sense of control over their health management. If the young person is encouraged to develop the skills necessary to self-manage their condition and be actively involved in communicating with their medics, they will be more likely to feel confident in dealing with the pressures of explaining their condition to their friends.[14] The young person should be encouraged to speak with confidence and from a position of knowledge. It is worth their talking about how to respond to questions with a parent or sibling before they talk to friends or peers. Role play can be used to practise scenarios and to increase confidence. For adolescents, having a sense of awareness of how others perceive them can be difficult to deal with. Children and young people can be self-conscious and feel alienated by their condition. Communication can help to eradicate feelings of low self-esteem, and to enable the child or young person to address negative emotions.

Friends will want to know how to help and be supportive, but will be unsure of how to do this – encourage the young person to let them know what they would like them to do. Friends can help the child or young person stay in touch with their school by relaying information and updates on the school news. They can also help them stay up to date with school work.

The young person should tell friends that their chronic illness is one aspect of their life, not their whole life – they are still the same person, with the same interests and personality. Sharing information about the condition and treatment is helpful. Friends can be frightened and worried but unable to address their concerns for fear of causing distress. If the young person can be open about their condition, they will be able to address their friends' concerns. Through communicating information and knowledge, myths about chronic illness can be tackled. Inform the peer group that the illness is not contagious and that not all chronic illnesses result in an early death.

Maintaining friendships is difficult when the young person has to spend periods of time out of school or in hospital. Texting, instant messaging, email and websites are all effective communication tools to enable young people to stay in touch.

Friends and teachers should be encouraged to visit when the young person is in hospital or too unwell to attend school. Maintaining contact with school and friends can provide an easier transition when the child or young person is ready to return to school. It is useful to establish an interest or activity that can be shared with peers, but which does not require the young person to over-exert themselves – for instance, video gaming and computer technology create an equal playing field for a young person who is physically limited.

❖ Advice and action points ❖

- *Discuss* with your partner or child concerns that you wish to raise at consultation appointments. Through spending some time in advance of the appointment thinking about what you want to know, you will be better prepared and will make better use of the appointment time.

- *Identify* a key family member or friend to disseminate information on your behalf during hospital stays. Making endless telephone calls is tiring and expensive.

- *Respond* to your child's need for information. Use books written for children about their condition, access websites for children with a chronic illness and encourage your child to ask their medical team questions.

- *Encourage* your child to discuss their concerns with their health team. This helps them foster a relationship and allows them to

ask questions that they may feel uncomfortable asking a
parent.

- *Create* your own information pack with relevant contact
  numbers of doctors, pharmacists, teachers, social workers, etc.
  Include an emergency page with information for babysitters or
  grandparents on what to do should an emergency arise.

- *Share* information with other parents – it is amazing what you
  can find out to help each other.

- *Create* a family journal or scrapbook, which can be used as a
  talking point for the whole family. Include photographs and
  keepsakes from special outings and holidays, and look over it
  together as a family during times when outings are restricted
  because of your child's illness.

- *Talk* about how the illness or condition affects the whole
  family. How can you lessen the impact and help each other?

- *Discuss*, as a family, ways in which to support the child with a
  chronic illness. Encourage siblings to talk about the illness
  with the child.

- *Ask* for an intermediary if communication with the health
  professionals breaks down. Social workers or child life
  specialists can advocate for your child. Keep a diary or journal,
  and jot down appointment times and test results.

- *Ask* one of the medical team to spend some time explaining
  and discussing test results with you and, if appropriate, your
  child.

- *Be* honest and direct with your child when they ask questions.
  Remember they need information to be able to communicate
  with their peers.

- *Keep talking* as a family – remember siblings and grandparents
  need to be informed too. Family discussions will help release
  tension.

- *Create* opportunities for your child to socialize with their peers. Help them educate and inform their friends through communication about their illness.

You now understand the importance of good communication and the benefits of sharing information. Knowledge can eradicate fear and ignorance, and good communication is necessary to disseminate information. Talking with the medical team can help ease your worries and help them do their job.

4

Support: Where to Turn for Help

Parenting a child with a chronic illness is a long, tiring process. To manage the new reality of living with chronic illness, the family will need support from a network of services and people in order to adjust to the demands placed on all family members. If the family is supported, the child with a chronic illness is more likely to have a better quality of life and a better chance of reaching their full potential. To achieve good and effective support, the parents need to be able to identify the type of help they require and then to access services or individuals who can fulfil those requirements.[1]

Identifying and accessing support is not always straightforward. Some parents are limited by the geography of where they live, and rural families often experience increased isolation from services and support. Other families find that the amount of energy and motivation required to make contact with outside agencies or social services is too great. They are overwhelmed by the demands of the chronic illness and unable to initiate support. Catherine Murnin, from the Child Brain Injury Trust (CBIT), believes that families do not always have the skills necessary to access support. They depend on organizations like CBIT to negotiate community therapies, to work with schools and to explain benefit entitlements:

> Families need support to provide routine and consistency in all aspects of the child's life. Changes occur day to day as the child

> grows and develops and parents need to put procedures in place for the long term. We advocate that parents are given our information at the diagnosis stage with a follow-up point of contact.

Organizations like CBIT provide a bridge between statutory agencies and families.

Research has highlighted that children with chronic conditions face emotional, developmental and educational difficulties. Social support, both organized and informal, does help families to cope.[2]

The impact of the condition on the child's and the family's everyday life may unfold gradually. The family can become accustomed to the difficulties more easily if they are incremental and not sudden. For many families, the changes occur overnight and the involvement of many individuals, agencies and professionals is required to aid the family and help them to cope. While there are common factors in how chronic illness affects a family, support needs to be designed to suit the individuals concerned. Care and support must be relevant to the family's needs or it risks being intrusive.

Support within the hospital setting is largely concerned with clinical and medical provision. Increased awareness of the need to support families in their care for the child at home has led to the emergence of statutory and voluntary agencies designed to work in partnership with the family and health system. More children with chronic conditions are having their care managed at home than ever before. To meet their needs, care packages designed to be implemented by community practitioners are more common.

Some children leave hospital dependent on medical equipment. Parents need to be trained to operate the equipment and to be able to manage the child's healthcare needs. A good support network is essential to help the family cope with the medical technology. The child's life may depend on the equipment, which means it is not easy for the parents to leave the child with other family members unless they too are fully trained in managing the equipment. The parents must be organized to ensure that they have regular supplies of the medical equipment being used. They may need catheters, swabs, sterile needles, hazardous waste disposal bins, feeding tubes, suction equipment and rubber gloves among other things. The equipment must be maintained and checked regularly by professionals. Unfortunately, the financial cost of caring for a child dependent on medical technology can be huge and, in some healthcare systems, issues of how to meet such costs can put the family under more stress.

Parents are subject to repeated periods of heightened stress when caring for a child with a chronic illness. The diagnosis is the first of many such times; moving from the hospital environment to care for the child at home also marks a time of heightened stress. The family are required to adapt to the demands of caring for the child without their medical team on hand. In hospital, home life can seem suspended with chores forgotten or assigned to those providing support but, when the family returns home, they are often expected to continue caring for the child and maintain their regular demands of home and work.

Sometimes the home or the child's bedroom needs to be adapted to make room for the equipment. Children dependent on medical technology may need regular nursing care. While being a source of support, nurses who call on the child throughout the day can also cause a strain on the family because they feel they are always playing host. They are never alone as a family and have to adapt to living with a loss of privacy.

The family needs long-term clinical care, emotional support and advocacy when dealing with the multi-agencies (government financial and social benefits). They also require support and understanding from the child's school or place of learning. There are resources available to help families but identifying needs and seeking support before crisis times are crucial.

We have established that the diagnosis period is followed by a period of readjustment. The family begins to adapt and create a new order which incorporates the demands of the illness into everyday life. Parents may need to take time off work or work flexible hours. The child with a chronic illness may be absent from school for periods and home schooling may be required. Siblings, too, often miss school days due to the constraints of travelling to hospitals and treatment centres. Over time, the day-to-day management of the medical condition becomes woven into the routine of family life but, to ease this transition and ensure that there is back-up support during crisis periods, a network of supporters is required.

Support must also be emotional. When a child becomes ill, the parents can experience a sense of failure that they have in someway failed to protect the child. Emotional support from family, friends and health professionals needs to address this sense of failure and to help strengthen the parents' self-esteem. Talking about the impact of the illness on a parent's sense of self-worth is useful. Those offering emotional support should help the parent to see how they have coped with the child's condition prior to the diagnosis. Often the diagnosis brings with it the opportunity for action to help the child in the form of treatment. The parent should be encouraged to view the diagnosis as a positive step towards helping the child's condition.

Chronic illness can last a lifetime and support must reflect the longevity of the condition. Families need help with adjusting to the condition, planning for the future, working with health and social services and co-ordinating their child's educational needs. Support needs to be available at the earliest possible opportunity and to be stepped up at times of crisis. While everyone copes differently and utilizes differing coping mechanisms, most families find that they rely on their extended family for their ongoing support.

The core medical team is supported by occupational therapists, pharmacists, physiotherapists, play therapists and social workers among others. There is a network of people working to support the child with a chronic illness. Outside this health service network are the family support workers, charities, support groups and other social groups. Beyond this is the extended family unit, friends and neighbours. They will all be valuable in their support at some point in the child with a chronic illness's life.

As difficult as it is to stay in hospital, they are also places where families can feel 'looked after' and safe. At home, care creates new stresses and places a huge responsibility on parents to carry out often difficult and complex medical procedures. Even managing appointment schedules, medicines and physiotherapy can be stressful. The transition from hospital to home requires help from many community practitioners to ensure that the child with a chronic illness is well cared for and the family able to cope.

It is a challenge for the family to adapt to normal family life at home. Even when the child has a well period or a period of remission, there are still demands placed on the family to ensure that the child stays well. The daily demands of family living go on. Children need to have homework supervised and gym kits packed, and parents need to go to work. Without a network of support, these tasks become impossible. Research has shown that families with strong support cope better than those without.

Chronic illness has been described as a whole family experience. Parents, siblings, grandparents, aunts, uncles and cousins are all affected. The child has a role within the extended family unit and in most normal functioning families they have developed relationships with their family members. Family gatherings and celebrations can seem hurtful if the child with a chronic illness is too ill to attend. On the other hand, the extended family is perhaps best placed to make adaptations to the party to suit the ill child – venue, food, etc. can all be chosen to suit the needs of the child.

All families experience periods of disharmony. The diagnosis of a chronic condition does not necessarily mean that differences will be resolved overnight. Some families become stronger and work well in supporting each other. I was amazed and grateful for the ongoing support we received during Owen's illness from both sides of the family (the Copeland and Dempsey clans). Their need to feel close to Owen was often translated into practical help.

Unfortunately, some families are incapable of pulling together and become alienated. Resentment can build when the parents of the child with a chronic illness do not feel supported by their extended family. Often poor communication is the cause. As one mother found, her extended family did not realize how serious her child's condition was: 'Some family members didn't see the significance of the illness or the gravity of the situation so their support was limited, much to my frustration and annoyance.'

Family members may feel reluctant to help for fear of taking over or becoming too involved. Some are simply frightened and, in not knowing what to say, choose to say nothing and so appear uncaring. The parents of the child with a chronic illness may feel envious of the lives of those close to them who appear carefree and happy, or become angry when other family members complain about normal family problems. In comparison to the gruelling demands of caring for a sick child, problems caused by teenage rebellion seem insignificant.

Different people are better equipped for offering different types of support. One family member might find it difficult to express how they feel about the child's illness but spend time doing chores and visiting the child in hospital. Another family member may seek to support the family emotionally by talking about the illness and the impact on the family. Recognizing who to turn to in times of need is part of the learning process at the time of diagnosis. It soon becomes apparent who the family can rely on not just during times of heightened crisis but throughout the child's illness. Unfortunately, some people seem to thrive on the drama of a crisis situation and disappear during lulls when help is still required. Parents learn to recognize those who are genuine in their care and those who are less so.

The majority of care for the child with a chronic illness occurs at home. Often parents are expected to carry out medical care for their children who have complex needs. Most patients with a chronic illness do not spend a large proportion of time in hospital; treatment is often administered in short sessions if possible and the child can return home. Special equipment may be required to adapt the home to the child's abilities. Home care is considered preferable to most families to staying in hospital, but it can be an added strain. It is also a more cost-effective option. Special routines need to be created around the medical needs of the child or young person that affect the entire family. When the child returns home, the parents need to be able to deal with their medical needs. The mother of one child who had a central line fitted to have chemotherapy administered felt that in dealing with her child's complex medical needs she gained a sense of control:

> I liked looking after his Mr Wiggly as we called it. I had to flush the line, keeping the conditions sterile. While it was a big responsibility to make sure the line didn't become infected or blocked I felt that I was doing something to help him. It helped my self-esteem to be able to do something medical for him.

One father felt differently about medical care being carried out at home:

> It took away from his sense of normality and his freedom. Even though we were at home he had a constant reminder of his illness and the hospital. I didn't mind doing the medicines and looking after his medical needs – I would have done anything for him – but I hated that he had to be constantly aware of his illness.

The impact of the illness on the family is far-reaching. Changes range from lifestyle choices and work patterns to the layout of the home for disabled access. The dynamic of the relationships change – the youngest family member may be used to having special attention and extra help but when an older sibling is diagnosed with a serious condition the attention can swing away causing resentment.

Psychological support

It is apparent that a chronic condition, which affects a child physically, will also impede on their psychological wellbeing.

An illness that affects appearance, mobility, lifestyle, social interaction and general health will have an impact on the psychosocial aspects of the child. There is evidence to show that psychological support for children with a chronic illness can improve quality of life and help improve physical health.

Parents can benefit from talking to a psychologist to help guide them with parenting issues. It is easy to be over-protective of a sick child and to over-indulge them; talking to a psychologist will help the parent work out strategies for dealing with the child.[3] If the parent does not set limits, the child will believe the parent is no longer in control. All children need security and consistency. Problems with siblings can arise if the child with a chronic illness is perceived as being exempt from normal chores and family rules.

Balancing the need to parent the child in a 'normal' way while feeling a sense of injustice that the child is impeded by their condition or treatment is a challenge. It is easy for the parent to try to compensate for the child's illness by being lenient and indulgent. While the child with a chronic illness needs extra care, they also crave normality and the security that comes from routine and boundaries.

Parents can feel empowered by talking to a psychologist about such issues. Early on during Owen's treatment, we found it very difficult to enforce our normal bedtime routine. We felt that, while Owen obviously needed rest and a routine following his neurosurgery, we were somehow wrong to try to go back to our normal family routines. A chat with a psychologist helped us to understand that we needed to provide Owen with the security of our normal parenting skills for his wellbeing and his sense of normality. Many hospitals offer psychological support in the form of clinical psychologists, child life specialists, social workers and family support workers. Psychological support can assist parents in helping their child reach their potential and lead as normal a life as possible.

Hospital social workers and child life specialists can be of enormous help both psychologically and in practical terms. Their role is to help the family adjust to the demands of the diagnosis, cope with hospital and treatment protocols, and offer assistance with financial concerns. Some hospital social workers are employed by associated charities. This is also the case with family support workers who spend time with the families at home, helping with household tasks and looking after siblings or the ill child. Hospital social workers also offer advocacy, helping the family deal with the medics, employers and educators, and manage finances.

Families need to have a key person, responsible for co-ordinating their needs and assisting with advocacy. This single point of contact can be the social worker or child life specialist. When support is needed, there should be a fast-tracking system in place to meet the family's needs in a timely fashion. Crisis situations require immediate practical support. A lack of provision for psychological support for children with a chronic illness has been identified.[4]

While it has been recognized that children with a chronic illness will have a greater likelihood of suffering from depression or mental health problems if they are not supported, there is insufficient provision in place to facilitate such support. If the family has a social support system, then they are more likely to adjust to the demands of the condition and cope better.[5]

One of the greatest sources of support comes from other families experiencing the same type of condition. Friendships made on hospital wards are important to the entire family. While the extended family and friends can care and be involved, they do not truly understand. Hospital friends or friends made through support groups can also give advice and hints on dealing with the condition. Hospital social workers will be able to provide a list of support groups and relevant charities. We still remain in contact with friends made during Owen's hospital stays. His friendships formed over video games on the hospital ward helped to enhance his self-esteem and provided him with entertainment during hospital stays. The families of his friends became our friends, offering mutual support.

The financial strain of coping with long-term health problems is often under-estimated. Hospital stays are costly: car parking charges, paying for meals, extra treats and toys for the child, and paying for babysitting for siblings or after-school care all add up. Some charities offer financial support in the form of grant payments to cover travel or utility bills. The social worker should be able to contact the charities on behalf of the parent. Support for holidays and mini-breaks is also offered by some charities. Many charities run their own holiday accommodation or summer camps. These holidays are a good opportunity for the family to recharge and relax away from the hospital environment but surrounded by people who have an understanding of the child's needs.

Play therapy is recognized as being beneficial in helping children to explore issues affecting them.[6] Chronic illness creates a great deal of change in a child's life. The fear of hospital procedures and the uncertainty of the future create anxieties that can be explored through play therapy. The central premise of play therapy is that through play the child can communicate unconscious and conscious experiences and emotions.

Most hospitals employ play therapists to assist children in preparation for surgery or treatment. Play involving toy hospital equipment and implements reduces the fear attached to certain procedures. The children are encouraged to act out hospital interaction and in doing so gain a sense of control over their situation. Some hospital play therapists have dolls with central lines fitted, which the child can access with a syringe to draw 'blood' – coloured water. The action of explaining to the doll that the nurse or doctor will insert the syringe into their central line to take some blood or to give them some medication helps the child to understand the procedure and trust the medical staff. The medical procedure becomes less intimidating if the child can play-act the scenario with the play therapist. Furthermore, if the child has misconceptions about a procedure, then through talking and play-acting the play therapist will be able to identify them and explain.

Child life specialists are specially trained to assist families to cope with the challenge of the hospital experience. Their role is to help the child and the family to adjust to the diagnosis and prepare for hospital interventions. They deliver emotional support through educational, developmental and therapeutic activities for the ill child and their siblings. Child life specialists recognize the stresses and challenges of long-term healthcare and help the family identify their strengths and devise coping strategies. They also provide consultation with the medical team regarding psychosocial issues.

Support for teenagers

Many young people with a chronic illness find themselves increasingly isolated because of their illnesses or their treatment. Support for adolescents needs to be far-reaching, incorporating their physical needs with their psychological and social ones.[7] This social isolation from their peer group can be damaging to their emotional wellbeing and to their development. Internet access is being used in some hospitals to encourage young people to stay in touch with their friends and school, thus creating a virtual support network (see Chapter 3, Communication: A Two-way Street).

Support groups enable teenagers to meet and socialize with other young people experiencing the same illness or treatment. They can be of immense support. Sometimes the young people will not acknowledge their condition or limitations, preferring instead to enjoy *not* having to explain. They experience a freedom in being able to socialize and interact with other young people who understand their health condition.

Families join support groups to dispel isolation, share suggestions for dealing with the illness and its side-effects, and talk to others who are living through the same crisis. Individual and family counselling can help address shifting responsibilities within the family, explore methods to improve communication, and help find ways to channel strong feelings constructively.

Support for siblings

The well siblings of children with chronic illness are often the forgotten victims in that they are insufficiently supported. Their needs are overshadowed by the greater demands of the sick child. A child undergoing intensive treatment, or living with chronic pain, will demand the majority of the parents' time and attention. It is inevitable that the well siblings will be relegated. As one sibling described the effect of having a brother with a chronic illness:

> You have to grow up a lot faster. It isn't that there isn't enough emphasis placed on your own needs, it is just that his needs were greater. Obviously he came before everybody. Everybody rallied together to be there for him.

Normal childhood illnesses affecting well siblings seem of little importance except when they have an impact on the child with a chronic illness. Parents of children undergoing chemotherapy live in fear of siblings contracting chicken pox because it is potentially fatal for immuno-suppressed children. Children with compromised immune systems are at risk if their siblings become ill. Sometimes siblings are required to leave the family home until their infectious illness has passed, and this would naturally cause some resentment and upset.

Research has shown that, while there are negative consequences of living with a sibling with a chronic illness, there are also positive outcomes such as enhanced closeness within the family.[8] Siblings tend to be more independent, self-sufficient and compassionate. The mother of a child diagnosed with Hurler's syndrome said, 'Many people looking in felt that the other children became much better people, more caring and understanding. In fact as a result two out of three of my children have pursued careers in the caring professions.'

Chronic illness causes well siblings to experience major adjustments to their lives. Siblings can experience fear and worry. They can feel responsible for the child with a chronic illness and experience guilt. They can also develop a fear that, although they are currently well, they will become chronically ill themselves or their future children will become ill.

Often the child with a chronic illness receives more attention than the well siblings. While this is unavoidable, it can cause resentment and jealousy. The well siblings may also experience disruptive changes to their home life: parents often spend time with the sick child in hospital, the family can experience financial difficulties, holidays can be disrupted or cancelled, eating out can be more difficult and special diets may be adopted – all of which have an impact on the well sibling.

Chronic illness can have a detrimental effect on the psychological wellbeing of siblings if they are not acknowledged as care givers. Often well siblings are required to assist in the care of their sibling with a chronic illness. The negative impact of living with a sibling with a chronic illness can last well into adulthood if the child does not receive support.

One family support worker who looked after siblings of children living with cancer said:

> Siblings can lose out because the parents have to concentrate on the sick child.

> Often siblings can't have friends over for sleepovers. There are so many restrictions placed on them. Siblings worry about their parents and don't talk about things that will make them sad. They need someone outside of the family, maybe a grandparent or care worker, to talk about their fears.

Younger siblings experience difficulty in being separated from their parents during hospital stays. When I asked my daughter Kate, who is now 12 years old, how she felt during Owen's lengthy treatment, she said in relation to being separated from her family during hospital stays when she was five years old, 'It was as if the brain tumour was stealing my brother away along with my family. The tumour was taking them all away from me. It was as if it was controlling everything.'

Kate regularly stayed with my parents during Owen's chemotherapy sessions because I would be staying with Owen at the hospital and Liam would be coming from work straight to the hospital ward. She had her own bedroom at my parents' house and she was particularly close to them and well cared for. Nonetheless she felt excluded from her family. To accommodate our need to move back to Belfast from Cardiff to be near our extended family for support, Kate had to change schools and begin to make new friends. While she coped well with the move, largely because she was used to regular visits to Belfast and she understood the serious-ness of Owen's illness, it was still a great deal of change to expect a five-year-old to deal with.

To support the well sibling, parents should be open and honest. If the sibling understands why family life is disrupted, they will be more likely to accept the situation. Parents should encourage the sibling to ask questions and feel secure in voicing their worries. Often well siblings experience a sense of guilt that they are well and active. Siblings can have conflicting feelings, at times resenting the extra attention the child with a chronic illness receives and at others feeling responsible and worried.

Parents often experience feelings of guilt about how the well siblings are treated during crisis times. One mother, speaking of her two-year-old daughter, said: 'I wasn't a mother to her. I just left her.' Support for siblings needs to be practical and emotional. One mother described how she was thankful that her well children had a good relationship with a care worker from an organization called Crossroads:

> The best thing I did was to take help from both the hospice nurse and Crossroads care. The Crossroads care lady became my brick and in fact seven years later still is. The children were very fond of her and she sewed badges on their uniforms, backed their school books and made them food. She took over my role as their mother and they are still very close to her.
>
> I thought initially that I could do it all myself.

Resentment can build and the siblings can feel that their lives are being damaged for the sake of the sick child. Communication is essential. The siblings need to feel that they are important and that their needs are not being over-ridden. Chronic illness has an all-encompassing effect on family life. As one sibling said:

> Everything at home was regimented. From such a young age I had to cope with so much responsibility. I think when I look back, I didn't so much lose out on my childhood, it was just different. I matured more than others my age. Responsibility and caring for him helped me accept his condition. There is maturity which develops which means you can put yourself in other people's shoes and develop empathy. I am going into social work as a profession but I have a sense that while wanting to help people I feel I can't do enough because I can't become as involved as I was with my brother.

Siblings can experience problems with their peer groups. A lack of understanding and a sense of being different can cause isolation. It is important that the sibling understands the condition and feels confident in explaining it to their peers and friends. Some children grow up with a sibling with a chronic illness without feeling alienated or different until they interact with peers. Outsiders are more aware of the differences and high-light them, causing the sibling to become conscious of being different:

> My brother's needs were second nature to me but when I was around other people my own age I realized then how different he was and how different my family was. I would have to care for him while they [the friends] would be out in the street, and my brother couldn't do things that their brothers were doing, my brother couldn't come out and play. You become aware of the real differences.

Siblings should be encouraged to visit the brother or sister who is chronically ill when they are in hospital. Being able to visualize the hospital environment during periods of separation is comforting. Many siblings worry about their brother or sister. They become anxious and underlying concerns can develop into behavioural problems outside the home. It is important to inform the sibling's school about the difficulties of living with chronic illness. Parents should highlight the disruption to family life that the well sibling experiences along with the emotional stresses.

In some families, the well siblings try to be perfect – they strive to be successful at school and well behaved at home. They worry about the pressures they see their parents under and try to compensate by over-achieving. Some siblings recognize the freedom of not being closely monitored by their parents who are occupied with the child with a chronic illness but, in responding to the need to not create further problems, they comply. One sibling said:

> I could have gotten away with a lot because there wasn't the same attention on me. I remember friends my age would have a set time to be home by. I never had that yet I was always home at a reasonable time – I knew myself when to go home.

Support groups specifically for siblings provide an opportunity for them to interact with others who understand. Siblings have the opportunity to socialize in a relaxed, safe setting. They are with peers who understand and appreciate the difficulties they experience. This can help counteract the feelings of isolation and of being different. It is sometimes useful to create a family scrapbook for the younger child to look at during periods of separation. The scrapbook can include family photographs and mementos to help them cope with missing their sick sibling and parents.

Infants and toddlers can be comforted by sleeping with a piece of clothing from their mother. The familiar scent is reassuring. For older siblings, being able to telephone their parents when they need to can provide a degree of security and reassurance.

Support from grandparents

Chronic illness is a long and often tiring process, and support from family and friends will wane. Grandparents, however, are often the most dependable source of support. They provide emotional and practical back-up, looking after the well siblings and keeping the household running. One single parent discovered that she could only rely on her parents for support: 'The majority of the support for us came from my family. My dad and my mum both took the diagnosis really bad but they coped for me.'

Grandparents are known to experience the same emotions at the time of diagnosis as parents. They feel anger and grief and often want to attribute blame, or they feel intense guilt that they are in the later stages of life and may be relatively healthy while they have to watch their grandchild experience health problems. The level of acceptance varies from family to family, but it is often more difficult for grandparents than parents to reach acceptance. If the grandparents are not actively involved with the child on a regular basis, then acceptance can be particularly difficult.

Grandparents can be intermediaries between the family and the extended family, updating aunts and uncles on the child's progress; this takes the burden of repeating the same updates to everyone living away from the parents. When grandparents play an active role in supporting the family, it appears that other family members tend to have greater involvement. They can spur aunts and uncles into action and help reinforce the support network.

At crisis points during the child's illness, when medical emergencies affecting the parents occur or if exhaustion takes over, the grandparents are sometimes required to stay in hospital with the child. Parents should explain to grandparents what to do in the event of an emergency. It helps if they are familiar with the child's physicians and attend clinic appointments from time to time. Their involvement on a regular basis requires them to be knowledgeable about the child's condition and medical needs.

It is useful if the grandparents take an active interest in the child's condition and to do so they need to be well informed and kept up to date about the child's medical needs. They can be more understanding and supportive if they have knowledge of the child's limitations and health problems.

Some older grandparents experience anger and guilt that they are nearing the end of their lives in good health while their grandchild has so much ahead of them. One mother talked to me about her sense of guilt for causing her parents so much stress and worry:

> They had a blessed life and I felt how dare this happen to them, they are in retirement – they should be able to live out their twilight years in peace without this which devastated them.

> I felt a responsibility for bringing this pain to my mum and dad – I was the child who brought it into their lives.

Owen had to have regular Glomerular Filtration Rate (GFR) tests to measure his level of kidney function because of the side-effects of one of his chemotherapy drugs. The test could be painful with a dye being injected into his vein and withdrawn a few hours later. To cope with the painful procedure, he often called upon my mother to hold his hand. We had a routine of going into the treatment room without her and Owen would shout 'Hold my hand, Nanny' at the precise moment when he needed her. At home, he often played 'hospitals' with her and would re-enact his clinic appointments, subjecting his *Toy Story* Woody doll to all sorts of medical procedures. Their relationship was special. Owen had someone other than me or his father with whom to feel secure enough to explore his hospital concerns. Both my mum and dad spent time with Owen playing and having special time together, and this provided him with distraction from his illness and enabled me to have time to do necessary chores or shopping.

Problems can emerge with grandparents becoming over-involved, spoiling the child with a chronic illness and causing resentment in other siblings. Such problems are remedied through good communication. Explaining that the needs of the other siblings are important and that the grandparents can play an active role in meeting these too helps them to understand. Grandparents can often feel helpless and anxious. They experience a double concern, worrying about the grandchild with a chronic illness and their own child.

Some families experience problems when grandparents feel justified in voicing disagreement over parental issues such as discipline. They may feel that the child with a chronic illness is being spoiled and pampered. A lack of understanding is usually the cause of such differences and, when there is ongoing involvement and communication, they come to realize the child with a chronic illness's needs are different. Grandparents need to listen to the parents and to respond sensitively to their needs. They need to appreciate that their advice, while well meaning, is not always welcome.

Often it is those closest to us who suffer the brunt of our anger and anguish. It is not uncommon for mothers and daughters to row during heightened tensions. Both parties should recognize that the stress of caring for a child with a chronic illness can cause irrational behaviour and an outpouring of anger. Conflicts can be resolved if the lines of communication are kept open.

All children need consistency and it is important for the child with a chronic illness to be treated in a similar way when the parents have entrusted them to the care of grandparents. A parent may limit a child's intake of junk food while the grandparent believes they are just giving them a special treat. If the child requires a special diet and the grandparents ignore the restrictions, then the child's health is at risk. Most grandparents and parents want the same thing for the child – relative health and happiness; when they realize this, they can work together.

Many grandparents speak of the special relationship they have with the child. They feel that their lives have been enriched by being able to play an active role in caring for their grandchild.

Support of the extended family and friends

We are all social beings, some more than others. We rely on our relationships with people to validate who we are and to try to help us understand how we feel. These relationships, while valuable at times of stress, can also break down when put under pressure.

At the time of diagnosis, there is often an influx of emotional support in the form of cards, gifts and visitors. This eventually calms down, leaving the family feeling isolated and lonely while everyone else seems to go back to their normal lives. At crisis times, friends and family may become supportive again, responding to the acute situation. When family and friends appear uncaring because of a lack of support, it can often be that they do not fully realize the impact of the chronic illness on the family. Communicating the family's needs is important. Parents should ask for help. Most people are willing to contribute in some way. It is necessary to be co-ordinated in managing the child's care and the help that is available in order to ensure a continuity of support. Without planning and co-ordination, families risk allowing their support to be crises-led.

Opportunities offered through work and education mean that more people move from their home towns and settle in new countries. Geographical isolation from the extended family can place an added strain on the family of the child with a chronic illness. The geographical distance between extended families has placed a much greater expectation on the core family unit to be independent. Grandparents, aunts and uncles are no longer a daily part of the child's upbringing for some families. This makes support and asking for help more difficult.

Families who have been used to operating as a core unit find themselves returning to their extended families and even moving to be closer to them during times of crisis. If this occurs, as it did with our family (my mother moved to Cardiff to help look after Owen's sister, Kate, for three months while we were in the throes of Owen's diagnosis, surgery and early chemotherapy before we returned to Belfast), then it is necessary to investigate the hospital in the town the family is moving to. The child's consultant and medical team will make the referral and ensure medical notes, test results, scans etc. are transferred. Treatment may need to be co-ordinated between the two hospitals to ensure an optimal travelling time. Moving following a diagnosis of chronic illness is yet another stress for a family.

One mother found it difficult to ask for help. She felt that in asking for support she would be admitting to not coping. She felt a need to have control over all areas of her child's life and could not delegate to family or friends. This puts the family unit under greater pressure. In realizing that asking for and accepting support is not failing the sick child, but instead ensuring that the whole family is cared for in practical and emotional terms, the parent can *gain* control.

Friendship groups are an important source of support for children. Children living with chronic illness often find themselves isolated from their peers because of repeated absence from school. Periods of sickness, disability and fatigue all create difficulties for children in social settings, making children that are chronically ill more vulnerable to being excluded. Psychological intervention to help combat the social exclusion of children is necessary and needs to bring together the child's educators, health professionals and parents.

Religious support

Religion or spirituality can be a source of support for many families, although research has suggested that their spiritual needs are often unmet.[9]

Spirituality has been recognized as a coping mechanism for children with a chronic illness and their families. Faith can provide meaning and a wider perspective on the illness, allowing the parent or child to find hope and strength. Some families gain strength through prayer and are supported in knowing that others are praying for them. The use of religious beliefs and spirituality as a support mechanism is regarded as positive and an active coping strategy.

Often those who are religious find their faith strengthened when they are confronted by chronic illness. Hospitals have chaplains who can talk to and pray with the family.

Many families gain emotional support from their congregation. The sense that a community is thinking of and praying for the sick child can be comforting and reassuring. Many congregations also offer practical support – for example, cooking meals and raising money for treatment or special treats for the sick child.

Spirituality and faith can help families to cope with the long-term strain of chronic illness. Believing that a higher power is supporting the child and the family helps to strengthen the resolve to continue.

Some people inevitably feel anger when their child is diagnosed with a chronic condition, and they may direct this anger at God. Religion can become a source of frustration when the parent feels that their prayers are not answered. It is also worth mentioning that some unscrupulous people prey on families in times of crisis, claiming to be able to cure the child through religion. If a parent is concerned that someone is making such claims and they feel uncomfortable or exploited, then they should discuss the matter with their clergy person.

Cure is different from healing. Healing involves an enhanced sense of life and enables the person to live with a sense of peace. Many people experience a renewal of their faith in times of crisis and find great comfort in believing that what we experience is part of a greater plan.

Many chronic illnesses such as psoriasis, chronic fatigue, eczema and asthma are concerned about living with maximum health and minimum interference. Other conditions such as cystic fibrosis, some brain tumours and cancers raise questions about death. Religion can provide a spiritual framework in which to discuss issues surrounding death.

Supporting your partner

All relationships need to be nurtured. Caring for a child with a chronic condition is demanding and often results in the parents' energies being directed to looking after the children's needs. Balancing the demands of work with family life and ongoing hospital stays or treatment can put the relationship under intense pressure. It is worth setting aside time in the day to talk to each other, if possible without the children. This may not always work out but making an effort to communicate is half the battle. It is useful to talk about positives instead of always dwelling on the problems or the worrying aspects. Life has a way of continuing even when during crisis periods.

Often parents take on distinct roles when a child is ill, with one caring for the child during the day while the other continues to work. Resentments can build up with one parent feeling that the other is unaffected by the child's condition. It is worth trying to see the situation from each other's position. For instance, the stay-at-home parent should try to imagine leaving the child each morning to go to work perhaps in a stressful environment with colleagues who do not know or understand the strains the family is under. The working parent should acknowledge the stresses and frustrations of carrying out routine caring for the child: the monotony of waiting in hospitals, the social isolation. Often by acknowledging each other's stresses, the parents can support each other and lessen the strain. Sometimes pre-existing problems in the relationship will surface and be exaggerated by the stress of coping. Speaking to a counsellor can help.

Some couples find that they work well together throughout the illness. One mother spoke with pride at how she and her husband coped during their son's illness:

> We were magnificent as a couple. We really worked hard, acknowledging what was happening. Throughout the illness we were very focused and very realistic; neither of us had any false hope.
>
> I never sensed any pulling in opposite directions. He [their son] needed us both and he needed us equally.

Sometimes one partner can experience denial, refusing to accept the new reality. Each will experience the emotional array at various times and this can cause problems: while one person is trying to be optimistic, the other may sink into depression. The symptoms of depression include recurring crying, insomnia, loss of appetite, loss of energy and lethargy. If a partner is displaying these symptoms, it is worth advising them to seek help from their GP.

Many relationships flounder because the partners have not communicated how they feel about their child's condition. How the parents handle the diagnosis period is crucial. Some people become introverted and avoid discussing their emotions. One mother told me her husband barely communicated with her for six months following their child's diagnosis. Some parents experience a sense of disappointment that their life and their child's life have been so altered.

It is important to respond to each other's needs for closeness, but also to give each other space to process feelings.

For further information on the effect a child with chronic illness can have on the parents' relationship, see the Contact a Family website at www.cafamily.org.uk/relationships.html.

Support in the workplace

For families living with the gruelling demands of caring for a child with a chronic illness, the inflexibility of employers is often a burden too far. Many families do not have the financial resources to opt out of work, take unpaid leave or employ specialist childminders who are trained to look after children with complex medical needs. Often it is lower-income workers who face the most problems when it comes to crisis times in the child's illness. Employers are becoming more aware of the need to offer flexibility. UK government legislation has provided for unpaid emergency time off work to care for a dependant. The amount of time depends on the emergency and should only be sufficient to deal with the immediate problem.

As all families living with a child with a chronic illness have found, this is just not enough. While some statutory provision is in place for parents of disabled children to request flexible working practices, not all employers are able to meet the needs of the family.

Working parents should request a meeting with their manager and human resources personnel following the diagnosis of a child's chronic condition. The parent should explain the demands placed on the family and, if necessary, ask for support in the form of flexible working practices. Technological advances have enabled some companies to support home working arrangements. The parent should discuss this as an option if it is appropriate to their job description.

Single parents face the added pressure of being the sole income provider and the primary carer. Often it is impossible for a single parent to continue working while looking after a child with a chronic illness. Social welfare benefits may be the only means available to a single parent family. The hospital social worker will be able to advise the parent on how to claim disability entitlements and income support.

Community support

There is a wide range of voluntary and statutory organizations and agencies set up to support specific conditions relating to disability. These organizations operate at a national and regional level, providing local support for families. Many of these organizations offer mutual support, peer mentoring, family activities and play sessions, information and counselling.

Some organizations offer practical help in the form of 'shared care' schemes. Respite care is provided by trained care workers, either in the child's home or in the carer's home. There are times when parents cannot continue offering intensive care and need extra support in the form of respite care. In the right environment, the child may also find respite care beneficial – they are being cared for by someone with enthusiasm and energy in a purpose-built facility. A weekend break can be an efficient way for parents to recharge, spend some time together and find renewed energy to care for their child.

While we never needed to access respite care for Owen, we were fortunate to have a Clic Sargent family support worker called Carol. She became a valuable friend, providing support for Kate, Owen's sister, doing hours and hours of ironing, playing with Owen and listening to me whenever I needed someone to talk to. Her training and awareness meant that she understood Owen's treatment and the restrictions of living with a chronic illness.

Charities host family activity days that provide entertainment for the family in a safe environment where they can meet up with other families experiencing the same condition. Families become part of a network of mutual support, sharing information and experiences. Regular newsletters produced by charities and voluntary organizations help to keep the families informed about the organization's activities and developments. There is a range of network support groups that seek to help families by linking them up with other families in the same situation. This mutual support is beneficial and helpful to well siblings as well as the sick child.

❖ Advice and action points ❖

- *Recognize* that the transition from hospital-based care to home-based care will have an impact on all family members, and can give rise to a period of stress while the transition takes place.

- *Prepare* the family for adjustments to the new routine. Discuss how the child with a chronic illness will need extra help and time, and work out how all family members can be involved.

- *Seek* support to adapt the home to meet the needs of the child. Adjustments may be minor with a designated medicine cupboard, or they may be significant with structural changes needed to accommodate a wheelchair.

- *Encourage* people to help. It is easy to feel isolated and alone but, by opening up to others, we can find commonalities and support.

- *Communicate* your needs, both practical and emotional. Friends, family and support organizations will all be able to provide help and support if you ask.

- *Acknowledge* the support you are given and show your appreciation. Individuals will be more willing to help if they sense that they are contributing to the welfare of the family and in particular the wellbeing of the sick child.

- *Collaborate* with medics, support groups and individuals to identify your family's needs and find innovative and creative ways to meet these needs.

- *Explain* to family and friends that, in helping to support you and your other children, they are in effect helping the child with a chronic illness. In holding your hand, they are holding the child's.

- *Be aware* of the limitations of others. Do not expect too much and you will not be disappointed.

- *Explain* that you will need those supporting you to be flexible in their help – no two days are the same.

- *Acknowledge* the love and support the well sibling is giving to their brother or sister.

Sometimes setting SMART goals (specific, measurable, attainable, relevant and timed) can clarify needs and expectations along with achievements. In setting goals, help and support can be more efficient and effective. It is worth telling family and friends how they can help. Be direct about your family's needs; give precise instructions as to what you need to be done.

Let those who are supporting you feel valued and appreciated.

Evaluate the support on offer and identify shortfalls. Raise concerns about the family's needs to the healthcare team and work together to enhance the support on offer.

The whole family lives in the shadow of chronic illness. They are all affected and, while some family members rise to the challenge and provide immense support, others, for whatever reasons, find they cannot participate. Identifying family members and friends who can be relied on and called on in times of crisis is important. Inevitably there will emerge a tight circle of special people who want to spend time with the child with a chronic illness, who recognize the need for the parents to speak openly and truthfully about their fears, concerns and frustrations, and who appreciate the necessity to support the siblings. These extraordinary people will themselves be affected by the child's condition, but they can take comfort in knowing that in providing support for the family they will be directly helping the child.

5

The Education and Learning Experience

The education experience is important for all children. School is concerned with more than academic learning – it is the social arena in which children learn to interact and form friendships. Children who are physically impaired can find great satisfaction in achieving academic success, and those who are not academically inclined can find great enjoyment and support through the social side of school.

School can be a release from the tedium of hospitalization. It can be a diversion and provide some independence for the child away from their parents. Often children with a chronic illness spend a disproportionate amount of time in the company of their parents and other adults. School enables them to interact with other children and to develop social skills and emotional independence.

In many ways school is a microcosm of society in general and, in interacting with teachers and pupils, the child with a chronic illness will learn how to present their illness outside school and experience how their condition is perceived by others. Common to the majority of children with chronic illness is the desire to be treated the same as their friends, and to engage in learning and normal school activities.

While there is a great diversity of chronic medical conditions affecting school-age children, there exists a commonality of needs that the school must meet. Children need understanding, vigilance and extra support during periods of weakness or crisis, and to feel included. Every child needs to feel part of their school community. They need to take part in sports, school fundraising, drama productions and school trips. There is so much more to school than academic endeavour. To reach a satisfactory partnership between the school and the family, it is worth identifying the child's needs and the parents' expectations as to how these needs will be met.

Sending a child with a chronic illness to school can feel a huge risk to parents who have been used to closely monitoring them. They are entrusting their child into the care of teachers, and the school environment can appear to be overwhelming and treacherous. Children with compromised immunity are at risk of infections and common childhood illnesses, children with dietary restrictions may be tempted to try forbidden foods and children with physical impairments may find it difficult to cope in the playground or be teased or bullied. School is important for a child's development both intellectually and socially. If parents work with the school and communicate effectively, they increase the likelihood of the child having a positive, enjoyable school experience.

Many parents feel that it is a lack of understanding on the part of school personnel and limited accommodation of the child's needs that, as opposed to the child's condition, are barriers to their successful return to school.[1] Children that are chronically ill can face exclusion through fear and ignorance of their condition in the education arena. Teachers may feel that the child is not able to participate in school activities such as stage productions, school trips, sports days and playground games. A lack of resources, financial and time, can prevent adequate training for teachers to provide good practice in teaching children with a chronic illness. Teachers can feel burdened by the responsibility of having a child with a chronic illness in their classroom, although any sense of burden will have been born out of a lack of understanding – the child would not be in school if they were unable to cope with the appropriate support provided. Teachers can feel that their job is to teach and that they cannot afford to address individual needs on an ongoing basis.

When a child has support from their school and feels included and part of the school community, their self-esteem and sense of wellbeing can be immeasurably enhanced. Owen's experience of school was extremely positive. Just before his fourth birthday, he began attending nursery school for two and a half hours each day. He engaged in play activities designed to stimulate his interest in topics such as science, nature, language development and creativity. While at the beginning he found it difficult to let me leave him, he made friends easily and enjoyed playing with his two best friends, Ciaran and Laurence. His teacher, Hester Graham, while being watchful and cautious, ensured that Owen had every opportunity to engage in outside activities. He was slightly underweight and less physically strong than his peers. On one occasion, I can remember watching from the nursery school window as he was trying to navigate a tricycle designed for two children to ride together. Owen was up front steering and pedalling, which required quite a bit of effort. Unbeknown to Owen, Ciaran, the passenger, was using his hands on the back wheels to help propel the tricycle forward. That gesture of support and team work illustrated the strength of the friendship. Owen's self-image and confidence were helped by Ciaran's unspoken caring and kindness.

Owen often missed school because of his weakened immune system due to his chemotherapy and, when he couldn't attend, his teacher ensured that he was up to date with all the school news. He regularly saw, Ciaran and Laurence outside school, which helped to ensure that the friendships remained when he returned to school following his periods of illness.

By the time Owen began primary school, his tumour had returned and spread to his spine. Although he was relatively symptom-free for five months, he remained at home and continued his education with the help of a wonderful teacher called Margaret Rolston. His relationship with Margaret was special; she ensured that he remained in contact with his primary school and she provided a sense of continuity by bringing Owen books and activities that his peers were using in class. When his class was being visited by people who were involved in animal welfare, she and Hester Graham organized for them to visit Owen at home. We had many entertaining sessions with bats, hedgehogs and owls coming to our house.

On one occasion, Laurence came to visit Owen at home. By this stage Owen was extremely ill, dependent on steroids and morphine to control his headaches. He had not been able to attend school for several months but he asked Laurence who was sitting in his chair in class. I waited, frozen in anticipation of what Laurence would say, but was so relieved and delighted when Laurence replied, 'No one, it is empty, waiting for you.' We greatly appreciate the gesture of the primary one teacher, Orla McKenna, in keeping Owen's seat free for him to return to. I never thought that Owen would ask such a question, but it was obviously important to him to think that he would be returning to school. We discovered from Laurence that Owen's name was called out every morning at roll time and that the class regularly prayed for him.

When Owen's class were involved in the school nativity play, Owen was given the part of a shepherd along with Ciaran and Laurence. His music teacher, Karen McKenna, gave him a tape of the songs to be performed so that he could practise at home. We have special memories of that day when Owen played his part with great enthusiasm and stole the show with his irrepressible urge to dance while he sang the Christmas songs. He felt part of the school community and he was able to cope with his absences from school knowing that his teachers and friends still thought of him and included him when he was well enough.

School-age children with chronic illness can suffer the added burden of feeling less confident and less motivated than their peers. Repeated absence from school and the effects of the illness on their abilities can all reinforce feelings of isolation and insecurity. A good working relationship with the school can actively enhance a child's self-esteem. Some children can face difficulty in communicating or in establishing friendships. School can be an added pressure and source of frustration. It is necessary for parents and educators to work closely to create a supportive environment in which the child can develop and flourish both academically and socially.

There exists a great variation between schools in how responsive and supportive they are to children with a chronic illness. Some schools, such as St Joseph's primary school where Owen was a pupil, are exemplary in their care, while others display a complete lack of appreciation of how important their role is to the child.

A successful school experience can be achieved through good communication between the parents, the medics and the educators. Collaboration ensures that the child's needs, both medical and psychological, are understood and met. Understanding on the part of the school enables the child to have a full school experience.

Every child is an individual and, while schools can adopt generalized policies for working with children with different needs, they must also work in conjunction with families to ensure specific needs are met. Children that are chronically ill require individualized pathways and protocols, and it is imperative that the school understands the need for ongoing communication with parents to ensure that they are meeting the needs of the child.

The child with a chronic illness can experience a multitude of problems in school caused by the limitations of their condition or repeated absence due to illness or hospital stays. The child can be isolated from their peers because of physical differences, making interaction in the playground challenging. The child with a chronic illness can feel alienated and set apart from their peers. Their life experience is very different from other children: they may have experienced illness, pain, the trauma of surgery, problems with body image or intellectual impairment. However, the child can learn to cope with the challenges they face and be better prepared for life beyond school.[2]

Repeated hospital stays and treatment can affect a child's morale and self-esteem. They can feel isolated and stigmatized by their condition. When the school is a supportive environment, the child's self-esteem can be greatly enhanced and they can feel valued as a member of the school community. To achieve this sense of belonging and extract the best for the child out of the learning environment, the parents and the school staff must work together.

Problems can arise for children with a chronic illness attending school when their illness is intermittent. A child living with myalgic encephalomyelitis (ME) can experience periods of relative wellness and then be overcome with symptoms ranging from exhaustion, neurological problems, memory retrieval problems and difficulty in concentrating. A teacher can interpret the sudden display of symptoms as being evidence of laziness or boredom. Some teachers may mistakenly believe that the child with a chronic illness is 'playing up', looking for attention or trying to avoid work. Most children that are chronically ill simply want to fit in. They do not want to draw attention to their condition or to be treated differently from their peers.

The school needs to be supportive during periods of active disease and periods of remission. Periods of remission may be symptom-free, but the child and the parents are constantly vigilant, looking for signs of recurrence. Teachers can be aware of symptoms that could indicate the return of the disease. Educators become part of the child's care team. When a child spends up to six hours a day, five days a week, in school, it can be the teachers who notice the onset of fatigue, headaches, blurred vision, nausea, episodes of breathing difficulty, abdominal pain or toilet problems. A well-informed teacher will be able to read the signs and know when to contact parents or to work with the child and allow them extra time with work or one-to-one assistance.

Children who spend long periods of time in hospital often attend hospital schools. While being a welcome interlude in the day for parents and the child, they are often limited in what they can offer the child academically. The hospital school teachers have no connection with the child's school and therefore no sense of how the child is achieving. Classes on hospital wards are small or one-to-one, but of mixed ability and mixed age. There are limited resources and no provision for linking in with the child's school. The hospital school does not allow for social integration or sporting activities. While being useful for the child during hospital stays, the hospital school can be limited in what it can offer.

Advances in technology are enabling children to link in via web access with their schools. Online access to the child's classroom means that the child's educational and social needs can be more fully met. Regular contact with the school, in person, through video-conferencing or online, allows the child to feel connected, to be part of their class group and to be acknowledged during their absences. Continuity of education in this way allows for an easier return to school. The child will feel less intimidated and anxious about returning when contact has been ongoing (see Chapter 3, Communication: A Two-way Street).

Parents need to create opportunities for the child to remain in contact with their school, with academic developments and social and sports activities. The school experience is more than just academic study and the child will need input from their peers to remain socially part of the school community. When parents have been used to caring for their child intensively, it can be difficult for them to relinquish their child and allow them to go to school. One mother described how her child's special needs school became a place of support for both of them:

I did not want the child to even go to a special school but I soon realized how selfish this was of me. He deserved to have his own life and friends apart from the family. He loved school and the teachers were great. I was launched into a world of handicap and I was terrified at first. I very quickly realized it was the most beautiful world and full of very lovable and special children. As parents we supported each other and understood each other very well.

When a child has spent long periods of time out of school, either staying in hospital or at home during illness, returning to school can be traumatic. The child with a chronic illness can experience anxiety separation. They spend most of their time with their parents and find that being separated makes them feel fearful and insecure. If the fears persist and the child becomes withdrawn and anxious, they may need to be referred to a psychologist to help them work through their worries. The child who has regular contact either through visitors or written communication from friends and teachers will find reintegration to be less stressful.

Advocating in the school arena

Personal contact with the school is important. If the child has been a pupil before the diagnosis has occurred, they may find the school more responsive in offering help and support. The school and pupil will already have formulated a relationship and their shared history can be a platform on which to negotiate future involvement. When a child becomes ill or has had an injury, the school are often supportive – teachers should visit the child in hospital and often the pupils send cards and presents. This type of involvement enables the child to feel important to their peers. Their self-worth is often threatened by chronic illness and contact from fellow pupils can help them feel that their school friends care.

Unfortunately, not all educators are receptive to learning about a child's illness. Teachers can feel swamped with the increased demands placed on them. Class sizes have increased along with paper work. Some teachers may also feel frightened to be responsible for a sick child, and they are not legally bound to administer medicines.[3] Their resistance to encouraging the child with a chronic illness to participate in the classroom is born out of fear and ignorance. They do not know what the child is capable of, how they are perhaps limited by their condition, and they are anxious about possible crisis periods. Parents can work with the school to overcome teachers' anxieties. Training and sharing of information can resolve and alleviate most fears.

Children living with chronic conditions should be able to participate in learning with their peers. They should enjoy the same opportunities and activities and will make a positive contribution to the school. A common problem that parents face is a general lack of understanding.[4] A teacher may feel that they know what epilepsy or diabetes is and be reluctant to further their knowledge, thinking that it is unnecessary. Teachers can also feel that, if a child who has suffered a trauma to their head and is left with an acquired brain injury has returned to school, they must be well. The child may look the same and behave the same, but there can be underlying problems regarding concentration, memory recall or fatigue. A child living with juvenile rheumatoid arthritis can have periods of wellness and yet relapse can cause fatigue and pain. The child may be able to attend school but need breaks to rest or assistance moving from one classroom to another. Teachers need to be well informed to be able to appreciate subtle needs.

Creating a relationship following the diagnosis can be more difficult. Schools are under intense pressure to perform. They are experiencing staff shortages and budget cuts and a less than caring principal may view the inclusion of a child with a chronic illness as one problem too many. Thankfully, legislation is in place to protect the child. The child has a right to a full education. The school must by statute meet their full educational needs. Nonetheless, choosing the right school for the child can be challenging for parents. They may want the child to attend the same school as their siblings, but issues surrounding the child's educational needs may prevent them from doing so. This can be difficult for the child because it can set them apart from their siblings and make them feel alienated.

It is useful for parents to devise an agenda of what they expect from their child's school.[5] If parents spend some time discussing how they envisage their child's school life to be, they will be better able to identify areas of weakness that need to be addressed. Parents need to have realistic expectations. Schools are working within the restrictions of local authorities, government policy and set budgets.

School does not have to be a negative experience for the child with a chronic illness. They can find refuge in learning and enjoy friendships that provide them with distraction from their health problems and limitations. Parents need to work with the school to help provide a smooth transition for the child from hospital to school. The school should identify one person to take responsibility for overseeing the child's needs. This person can be the child's teacher, assigned teaching assistant or someone identified as being responsible for children's health needs. The school and the assigned person need to have a brief history of the child's medical condition. They need to have an awareness of the problems the child has encountered and how to work with the child to enhance their school experience. If the child has special needs, physically or intellectually, the school should be aware and show the parents and the child how they hope to meet these needs. Any special dietary requirements should be catered for and, if the child suffers from a severe allergy like peanut allergy, then the school should adopt a nut-free policy and actively enforce it.

If parents feel that their child's educational needs are not being met, then they should request a meeting with the teacher and school principal. The school personnel and the parents need to work together to identify barriers and be creative in finding solutions. Often it is a lack of vision that prevents good educational support. Teachers may not have experience of working with a child with a chronic illness and may not understand how they can accommodate them. Sharing information between parents, healthcare providers and educators enables a more comprehensive pathway for achieving successful support for the child with a chronic illness.

Information about the condition, along with emergency information and telephone contact numbers, should be provided and made available to all staff members who come into contact with the child. For instance, in most primary schools there is one class teacher responsible for a class. There is often also a classroom assistant, who may be there to support the child with a chronic illness. Often there is a music teacher attached to the school who may be employed on a part-time basis; drama teachers and sports teachers may also come into contact with the child. The range of teachers is extended further at secondary school with a child coming into contact with up to ten teachers in any one day. It is not sufficient for the teachers to have a one-off introductory information session about the child – the imparting of information needs to be on a regular basis, relating to how the illness is being managed. Chronic illness is a changing process and schools need to be kept informed.

It is important that the school is encouraged to share information among staff.[6] It is not sufficient for one teacher to be informed and then in their absence for a problem to arise. The child may have several teachers and each should be kept informed of their condition and progress in school.

Most children with a chronic illness will experience a sense of feeling different. Their illness and life experiences can set them apart from their peers. This alienation is often heightened and intensified at school where children compete academically and on the sports field. Some secondary-level schools operate mentoring programmes. This is a positive way to support the child with a chronic illness trying to reintegrate into the school community. A designated pupil can help to advise, befriend and support the child or young person.

Children that are chronically ill, depending on the restrictions of their condition, do not always develop emotionally or physically at the same rate as their peers. They may have a stronger sense of emotional maturity yet lack confidence in their abilities. School can present challenges in that teachers often expect all the children to be at roughly the same stage of development. Parents need to help teachers understand their child's abilities and limitations. It is through strong advocacy between the parents and the health professionals that the school can learn how to best accommodate and support the child.

It is a fact that children with a chronic illness are often absent from school. This can be an intermittent few days off or it can be months or years of absence. Missing school will inevitably have an impact on the child: they will be likely to fall behind with the curriculum and they will find it more difficult to establish friendships. Parents need to help the child and the school to plan for their return following a long absence. The child needs to have support to resume school work and may need extra tuition to compensate for the time they have missed. A long absence from school can mean that the child feels like a new pupil to the school. They may have forgotten routines and regulations. The child needs to be aware of changes in the classroom or school – as the school term moves on, different sports are introduced for physical education, new peripatetic teachers may have joined the school, or a new pupil may have arrived. The teacher needs to go over school rules and regulations with the child so that they are familiar with boundaries and restrictions. They also need to remind the child of the lunchtime routine and work with canteen staff to organize any special diets.

Problems for the child returning to school can be exacerbated by the fact that before the diagnosis the child performed well at school. They return to school and find that their abilities are limited and they have missed out on a lot of learning. This can affect their self-esteem and confidence, making them reluctant to speak out in class and to integrate successfully. Parents can be assured that a school is supporting their child if they have good responses to requests for meetings. Teachers and principals who make the time to meet parents are more likely to be proactive in making any necessary accommodations for the child, rather than simply being reactive as problems arise.

Communicating with the school

Parents must provide their child's school with information concerning their child's illness or condition.[7] It is the responsibility of parents to ensure that the school has knowledge of what to do should an emergency occur. The first point of contact for the parent should be the principal. The child's class teacher should then be involved in any correspondence or meetings, and any further members of staff who have contact or responsibility for the child should be aware of their health needs.

It is not sufficient to have a discussion with the principal about the child's condition. Written information, detailing how the child is affected by their illness, the use of medication or treatment and symptoms to be watchful for, should be made available to the principal and then disseminated around the key staff members in contact with the child.

Teachers need to understand how the illness can have an impact on the child's abilities, intellectually and physically. While asthma or Crohn's disease, for instance, will not impede a child intellectually, they may find absences from school affecting their performance. If a child has experienced a night of sleep disturbance due to their condition, then their ability to concentrate in school the next day will be affected. Parents need to feel that they can approach the teacher, either at the classroom door first thing in the morning or by sending a note with the child, to explain any difficulties the child has experienced sleeping.

Most schools claim to operate an open door policy regarding communication with parents. The parents of a child with a chronic illness need to feel that the school welcomes such ongoing communication. It is difficult to maintain good communication if the school personnel are unwelcoming to parents. Unfortunately, some parents are made to feel that they are looking for problems. The teacher may perceive the child to be coping with school but the parents may have a different perspective and need to discuss their worries with the teacher. Teachers should be encouraged to listen to parents and to acknowledge their concerns.

Teachers often need more than theoretical information on the child's condition. Some conditions require teachers to be trained to administer injections or medications. Training for teachers dealing with children who require medication in school is essential. The parents need to help the teachers understand how the condition has an impact on the child and how they may be affected by their symptoms.[8]

Further training and learning about the progress of the condition and its long-term effects are worthwhile and can be undertaken by the school nurse or the child's community health team. Parents should encourage communication between the school and the child's medical team. Often the community practitioners take on the role of intermediaries between the healthcare team and the school. Collaboration provides a more comprehensive support system, providing the child with continuity of care and ongoing support.

Some parents find that they are reluctant to push the child academically. They may perceive the child to be less able than they are and avoid putting them under pressure to complete assignments or keep up with the rest of the class. To do so is a great disservice to the child. Each child should be encouraged to reach their potential and children who have missed work due to absence should have adequate support to help them catch up.

Likewise, teachers who allow children with a chronic illness to under-achieve are failing to recognize the importance of education in improving and strengthening the child's abilities to process information and improve their memory and concentration, which can often be affected by their illness or treatment. A teacher or parent who is over-protective undermines the child's abilities and prevents them from becoming independent, putting them at an even greater disadvantage. A child who feels that they are not expected to do as well as their peers will become less confident and experience a sense of worthlessness. If teachers are telling them that there is no point in striving to learn, then they will carry those feelings through into adulthood and feel that society considers them less able. A teacher's lack of motivational drive will become a self-fulfilling prophecy and the child will fail to achieve their full potential.

Children who are physically limited by their condition can gain a great sense of satisfaction in competing equally with their peers in academic performance. Their learning experience can enhance their self-esteem and boost their confidence.

Parents are often anxious about allowing their children to go on school trips, especially if they involve overnight stays. One parent found the school's support for her child, who had suffered a head injury, to be significant in helping to alleviate her fears when his class was going on a school activity trip. The child had an enjoyable time, participating in many outdoor activities: 'If someone understands his abilities and disabilities, it can make all the difference.'

Parents can work with their community health providers to devise an action plan for the school. An action plan would typically include contact information, a brief medical history, details of medicines required during school and medication taken at home, dosage and when to administer it, emergency provision – signs and symptoms and how to respond – along with information regarding special dietary needs, transportation and any personal toilet needs the child may have.

Not all schools have a school nurse, but those that do can utilize the nurse as the child's case manager. This allows for accountability to ensure one key person disseminates information regarding the child's condition and oversees the general wellbeing and adaptation of the child in the school setting.

In the UK, most children with a chronic illness will have a community healthcare practitioner, either a community nurse or the local doctor. It is useful if the community practitioner makes contact with the school to help co-ordinate information and establish a relationship with the child's teachers. The community practitioner can assess the level of communication between the family and the school and, if necessary, improve the flow of information. The community nurse can also offer alternative strategies based on their awareness of other children's school experiences.

Often the paediatric nurse will provide the school staff with some basic training. Children living with immunological food allergies such as peanut allergy depend on teachers to make quick judgements on their condition and to react in what can be life and death situations. Schools have a duty of care to protect children with potentially fatal allergies. Many schools enforce a nut-free policy to ensure that children with peanut allergy are not put at risk by other children. Communicating the need to maintain such a policy is important to the wider school community. Likewise, if a child is being treated with maintenance chemotherapy and is well enough to attend school, they must not come into contact with chickenpox. The school has a duty of care to ensure that all pupils are aware of the risk to the child. If a child does have chickenpox, then the parents must inform the school immediately.

Children find that in school they are required to explain their condition to their peers. Some children try to avoid discussing their condition for fear of being teased but inevitably others will find out and it is better to pre-empt problems. Hiding a condition makes it appear to be something to be ashamed of. A child needs to be comfortable with sharing the information and to achieve a degree of ease they need to be knowledgeable about their condition. Certain medications and treatment can alter a child's or young person's appearance. Steroids for instance will cause weight gain and, if the child's peers do not know of the medication's side-effects and understand why the young person needs them, then they may be unkind and cruel in teasing.

Adolescents returning to school can be self-conscious and anxious. School is an important social arena for a teenager and being accepted by peers is important for a young person's self-esteem. Difficulties in school can lead to problems of non-compliance with treatment and management of their condition. In an effort to fit in and avoid appearing different, a teenager with diabetes or coeliac disease can often be inappropriately relaxed about managing their diet. In communicating the condition to peers and increasing their understanding of the limitations imposed by treatment, the adolescent is more likely to manage their condition successfully.

Before the child returns to school, it might be appropriate for the teacher or school nurse to talk to the other children. Any information given to the child's peers should be approved first by the parents, and in conjunction with the child or young person. Confidentiality should be respected. If the child or young person approves of the teacher or school nurse explaining their condition to their classmates, then it can provide an opportunity for the children to discuss the condition or illness and ask questions without offending or upsetting the sick child. Misconceptions about illnesses such as cancer or diabetes can be addressed. Some classmates might believe the condition is contagious, and the teacher can reassure them and explain the condition before the child returns to school. A child may be physically altered by their condition or by their treatment. Children returning to school following chemotherapy treatment will often have hair loss. This can be shocking if the children have not been prepared and, by addressing the issue before the child returns to the class, they will be less likely to stare or make inappropriate comments. If peers understand the condition, they are more likely to be supportive. In fact, a teenager with diabetes should teach their friends to be vigilant of signs of hypoglycaemia.

Children and young people can find it difficult to discuss their condition with their peers. They do not want to appear different and strive to cope with their condition while trying to create some normality in their lives. It is useful for parents to discuss ways in which they can deal with the return to school and pre-empt questions.[9] They can help the child or young person to prepare answers and practise how they should respond. Sometimes peers are frightened to ask questions for fear of upsetting their friend or cause offence. The illness then becomes a source of unspoken shame with neither acknowledging its effects. It is better for the child with a chronic illness to address their friends directly, in an open and positive manner, and ask, 'Do you have any questions about my illness?' Undoubtedly their peers will have many questions and the dialogue will flow. If the child feels that their teachers or friends are being over-protective and not allowing them to be independent, they can say, 'Thank you for your help, but I think I can manage this task on my own.'

Parent–teacher conferences present an opportunity for parents to speak to their child's teacher and receive information on their performance and behaviour in school. If problems arise for the child with a chronic illness, the teacher should alert the parents immediately rather than wait for a scheduled conference time at the end of term or school year; if problems go unchallenged, then it is more difficult to address them. When there is good communication between the school and the parents, the parent–teacher conference should be no more than an update opportunity, providing a review over the previous period. Specific issues need to be addressed as they arise, not weeks or months later.

Home schooling

Episodes of flare-ups, treatment demands and repeated hospitalizations can be too demanding for a child to maintain regular attendance at school. Life for the child with a chronic illness can be a schedule of medication, blood tests, physiotherapy, hospital appointments and limiting symptoms. For some children that are chronically ill, home schooling is necessary.

To compensate, many children learn to work independently or with guidance from their parents, although it can be difficult to motivate a child to study without being in a classroom environment. One parent strived to create normality for her child with a chronic illness by ensuring that he continued with his studies during long periods of absence from school: 'I pushed him to study. I thought if he wasn't sick he would have to study, so I was convincing myself that he was going to get better and return to school.'

Chronic illness can require children to spend long periods of time isolated in hospital wards in order to avoid infection following treatment. Children undergoing transplant procedures, treatment for leukaemia, or other conditions such as severe burns, can have only limited contact with family to protect them from infection. The psychological impact of such isolation can be great. The children are coping with the symptoms of their condition, procedural pain and discomfort, and the emotional stress of isolation. Children experiencing isolation cannot attend school and face problems of re-entering normal life when they are recovered. They have experienced worry and trauma that their peers cannot relate to.

Research and development of computer-aided communication for children in isolation is ongoing. It is hoped that children who experience long periods of isolation in hospital will be able to access the outside world through computer programs. This will enable them to feel less alienated and to have some continuity of their relationships with friends and teachers.

Owen was home-schooled for just over a year. His tutor, Margaret Rolston, was a wonderful woman who inspired him to learn and was able to reassure him that he wasn't falling behind with his work. His competitive nature and desire to learn made him want to stay ahead of his classmates. Despite sparse attendance at nursery school, Owen felt very much part of the school community.

Medication and school

If it is possible, the child's medication should be administered before and after school hours. However, if the child needs to take medicine, use inhalers or inject insulin while at school, it is necessary to keep the teacher and any members of staff who are in regular contact with the child fully informed. The school needs to know the full name of the medicine, and have contact names and numbers for the pharmacy supplying it, information concerning the dosage and any possible side-effects, along with information on how the medicine should be stored.

The child's prescription will state the dosage and how often a medicine needs to be taken. It is worth photocopying the prescription for the school to hold in its records. Most schools require written instructions from the parent concerning medication. The parent needs to give explicit permission to the teacher to administer medicine to the child, and this should be in writing. The medicine itself should be clearly labelled with the child's name, dosage and the pharmacy details. The parent should provide the school with a supply of medicine and make regular checks on when the prescription needs to be refilled.

The teacher should have an incident book to record when the medicine was given and to log any possible side-effects or changes in behaviour. Certain medication can induce sleepiness and the child may find it difficult to concentrate.

❖ Advice and action points ❖

- *Believe* in your abilities to speak up for your child. In advocating on their behalf, you are enabling them to live a fuller life with dreams and hope for the future.

- *Encourage* your child to assert their identity beyond their illness. School provides them with an environment concerned with more than illness.

- *Teach* your child to be a good friend. Other children will respond to a positive, friendly manner and attitude.

- *Encourage* your child to develop hobbies, musical abilities, reading, art, computer skills, craft work, drama – interests outside academic school work, which are enjoyable pastimes to develop in hospital or during periods of illness.

- *Help* your child to accept assistance and support from others when they need it without feeling helpless or guilty.

- *Allow* your child to grow in independence and strive to reach their full potential. Do not under-estimate your child's abilities because of their condition. Over-protection can hinder your child and prevent them from developing and growing in independence.

- *Discuss* how your child can best explain their illness to their peers. Teach them to be open and responsive to their friends' questions, but to not tolerate bullying or teasing.

- *Engage* in dialogue with the school to provide preparation and planning to ensure your child and their teacher are confident about working together.

- *Identify* risky scenarios and plan for emergencies so that if they occur those responsible for the child can react promptly and correctly.

- *Contact* the school before your child is due to return or start a new school, and request an induction programme to facilitate their entry. Become familiar with the child's rights to education and how you can access additional educational support if the mainstream system does not meet your child's needs.

- *Ensure* teachers do not under-estimate your child's abilities or need for education.

- *Provide* the school with written information concerning your child's condition, medication and potential side-effects, and a comprehensive list of contact numbers for emergencies. Communication should be ongoing and open.

- *Ensure* that the school supports your child during periods of absence by maintaining regular contact through visits, emails or letters.

- *Have* realistic expectations of your child's abilities. If they feel pressured to achieve beyond their capabilities, their self-esteem will be greatly affected.

Children with a chronic illness should be encouraged to reach their full potential intellectually and socially, and school is an important environment in which they can learn and develop. It is also perhaps one of the few places where the child with a chronic illness can assert some independence and develop life skills.

6

Day-to-day Family Life

One of the greatest challenges of parenting a child with chronic illness is balancing their health needs with their right to be parented in a consistent, fair and loving manner. Chronic illness does not have to define the family. It is a significant part of family life and can at times dominate, but it is only one aspect of the child, not the whole of the child. The successful family is one that encourages independence of all family members and strives to enjoy family life. To ensure that the family can adapt to the demands of the chronic condition, family-centred care is essential.[1]

It is all too common to try to over-compensate for the child's health problems. Many parents find that they want to give their child everything to somehow make up for the deficit that fate appears to have bestowed. However, this is to deny the child the right to be treated as a regular member of the family. Their health needs may be different, complex and demanding but ultimately they need their mum and dad to parent them as a child first and foremost, not as a *sick* child.[2]

The demands of caring for a child with a chronic illness can wear parents down at times. Parents will feel stressed, anxious and worried, at some times more than others.[3] It is a challenge to try to ensure that the stresses they feel do not impede on the family's quality of life. Often this means incorporating the illness into normal family life and maintaining regular family dynamics as far as possible. The huge adjustments that families must make to accommodate living with chronic illness range from daily adaptations to the home life routines, changes in work patterns, with one parent often giving up their employment to care for the child, financial readjustments, marital stress, sibling rivalry and childcare problems. Normal family routines change to incorporate treatment, hospital appointments and hospital stays, and at times of crisis household management must be delegated to the extended family, friends or agencies.

A more severe condition can have a huge impact on the everyday life of the family. Normal family activities, which most people take for granted, can appear like insurmountable challenges for the family living with a child dependent on medical technology. Parents reassess their priorities and, even if they both manage to maintain their employment, they inevitably find their focus and drive in work are diminished. To be resilient and cope with the condition, the family unit must maintain a sense of normal functioning. The needs of the individual family members are important though often over-shadowed by the greater needs of the sick child. In recognizing that the well siblings are often overlooked, parents are able to readdress the balance and through good communication help to create understanding.

It is important to remember that, while the child or young person is chronically ill, they are also growing and developing and will experience many of the same challenges as their peers. The child should be able to experience life as it should be – unhindered by illness or treatment. If the child experiences periods of remission or relative good health, they should be encouraged to embrace the normality.

While the family living with chronic illness experiences a period of adjustment following the diagnosis, they can still experience fulfilment and contentment within their new normality of family life.

Families often strive to convey normality to those outside their home.[4] They try to minimize the impact of the condition on family life by maintaining normal family activities and routines as far as possible. While this is a positive coping strategy for some, it can be detrimental to others living with a more severe condition. Normalization of the condition may not always be possible and, if the child's understanding of their condition has been constructed to be normal, they may experience distress and alienation when they encounter situations in which their limitations become obvious or heightened.

Parents of children with a chronic illness can struggle to meet their child's physical, medical and emotional needs. The illness has an impact on the family dynamic and can cause strain between family members. While recognizing and addressing the demands of the condition, trying to create a sense of normality can help families to cope with the stresses and strains of living with the condition. Most parents strive to create stable and secure homes for their children, but chronic illness can undermine the foundations of family life by causing upheaval at times of crisis or by creating emotional or financial stresses. Long-term illness and repeated periods of hospital stays can become an emotional and financial drain. One single parent found that worrying about money was an extra cause of stress:

> It was more pressure thinking about money. My company paid me full pay while my child was ill; without it I couldn't have coped financially. It is the extra expense of pyjamas and clothes, toys and games. It all adds up.

Creative thinking and good planning are often necessary for finding solutions to everyday problems. Communicating with health professionals and other families experiencing similar difficulties can help to resolve difficulties. For instance, a child living with physical disabilities can find transport to be problematic. Solutions can be shared by talking with other families. One family may have experienced adapting their car to accommodate their child, or have accessed government help in the form of financial aid to help pay for a new car. Sharing information can be an effective problem-solving strategy.

Other families can offer advice on where to holiday, where to eat out or how to negotiate support from social services. Sharing information is also a good form of support. Parents can find empowerment through working collectively. They share an expertise in caring for their children and can influence healthcare policy and hospital management if they strive to do so. Families who seek and offer support to others in the same situation find that they are emotionally stronger and better able to cope with the stresses of everyday living.

All parents from time to time feel the need to spend time doing things outside the family routine. Taking time away from the sick child is not always possible or desirable but, if the parents can spend a couple of hours a week engaging in hobbies or sports, they can return home recharged and more likely to cope. In the short term, caring for a sick child is difficult and demanding but, when care is long term, it is necessary for parents to create diversions for themselves to prevent mental and physical exhaustion. Some parents need respite breaks more than others. For some, short breaks make the difference between coping and not coping. They return re-energized and ready to face the ongoing demands of caring for their child.

It is worth setting goals to increase levels of exercise, relaxation periods and socializing. In creating a life beyond the demands of caring for the family's needs, the parents are ensuring that their wellbeing and mental health are being protected. While working to safeguard the wellbeing of the mother or father, the needs of the child with a chronic illness are more likely to be fully realized and met through the parents' effectiveness and enhanced self-esteem. Some families living with chronic illness can experience social isolation, feeling alienated from their friends and neighbours. Their previous social network may seem irrelevant to their new lifestyle, which can be dictated by treatment regimes. They feel limited in their opportunities to create a supportive, social network. Emotional support gained through relationships and friendships outside the family can provide greater resilience and increased coping ability. Sometimes it is necessary to create new friendships, and the hospital ward is often the best place to form them. Support groups and outings organized by groups supporting the child's condition also offer the opportunity to meet up with people who have an understanding of the stress and strains of parenting a child with a chronic illness.

Creating special time with the other well children is also important. They need one-to-one attention from their parents. When the whole family is engaged in outings or activities, inevitably the focus will be on the sick child. If the well children can spend time with their parents alone, they can feel satisfied in having their parents' full attention. Other family members need to be acknowledged as being significant and valued. They will experience the normal problems of growing up but will have the added stresses of living with a sick sibling. Managing the needs of the whole family can be difficult but, with good communication and support from the extended family, it is achievable.

To cope with chronic illness means that the family has accepted the condition and the inherent limitations and demands. Families who have made an active commitment to adjusting their lifestyle and adapting are more likely to cope. At the time of diagnosis, families begin the process of transition. A new reality unfolds, which includes difficulties, limitations and challenges. While the process of adapting is going on, so too is everyday life. The parents have work commitments, bills to pay, other children to raise. Children still have birthdays, Christmas still arrives and holidays loom. Normal everyday life and celebrations can seem like an added burden. Good organization and planning can help ease the pressure of dealing with family celebrations.

Sometimes the parent of the child living with a debilitating condition or experiencing chronic pain wants to focus on the child alone. They do not want to have to think beyond medication times and hospital appointments. However, to focus solely on the illness is not good for the child or the parents. The child is much more than their condition. They deserve to experience family outings, picnics, trips to the beach, holidays and birthday parties. It may take extra planning and a lot of energy, but it will be worth it. The demands of planning trips and days out can seem overwhelming especially if the child is dependent on medical equipment but, in making an effort to engage in activities, the whole family can benefit.

Many charities and voluntary agencies provide entertainment and family activities for children with a chronic illness. It is often easier to attend an event that has been planned by an organization that understands the child's needs. Such an event also provides an opportunity for families to meet others living with the same condition. They can provide emotional support and a network of friends who have shared experiences and can relate to their circumstances. Many families feel safe attending events organized or hosted by organizations connected to their hospital or local charity because of their awareness and support.

One father described the benefit of family activity days organized by Clic Sargent for children living with cancer: 'There is no need to explain our child's illness. Everyone is in the same boat and you know that no one will come with an infection.'

Activities that we all expect to take for granted can seem difficult and stressful when a child has a limiting health condition. Children living with skin conditions can feel embarrassed taking part in activities such as swimming. The mother of a child with severe eczema said, 'I didn't know if people would think he had a contagious rash. I was anxious and he was stressed. In the end he only spent a few minutes in the water.'

For the family living with chronic illness, family life is more complex than most.[5] The parents of a child with a chronic illness can feel resentful that life seems to be little more than scheduling medication rotas or applying new dressings before bedtime. Yet they still have hopes and dreams for their family and face ongoing demands on their time and finances. Chronic illness may dictate that the family is more organized in order to achieve good management of the condition. The need to schedule hospital appointments, treatment, medication and management of symptoms may mean lifestyle changes for the entire family. When the care for the child occurs largely at home, the family may feel that their lives are dictated by careful preparation and planning. However, it is possible to find a balance between managing the illness and coping with the demands of everyday life, while making time to enjoy life.

The impact of the condition on everyday life is often related to the severity and type of condition and the age or developmental stage of the child. A parent of an infant will find difficulties that do not relate to those encountered by a teenager. Similarly, a child living with moderate asthma will not require the same level of care as a child living with cystic fibrosis. If the family avoids social occasions and has limited recreational time, then they will become isolated and be at risk of developing mental health problems and depression. It is important to spend time together as a family without the illness being the focus. The child with a chronic illness will enjoy activities that allow the whole family to participate and interact. Good organization, scheduling of treatment and planning of family time can provide time to carry out family responsibilities.

Sometimes parents need to be resourceful. When a child is susceptible to infection or has a low immune system, creating fun outings can be difficult. They may not be able to socialize with other children for fear of infection, and visits to the park or the local swimming pool may prove too risky. When Owen was receiving chemotherapy, he was often immune suppressed. I contacted the local leisure centre and asked to book the bouncy castle for him and his sister to play on. The manager of the leisure centre offered us use of the bouncy castle before or after parties. Owen and Kate could enjoy a half hour of play outside the home without risk of

Owen coming into direct contact with other children who may have had colds, coughs or chickenpox and other childhood illnesses.

For us, keeping Owen infection-free was a priority. He spent a lot of time in hospital receiving chemotherapy and then, when he was at home, he often felt ill and weak as the side-effects took up to a week to wear off. As a result, we did not want him to have to be hospitalized because of preventable infections. While we could not control the cancer, we could be active in trying to prevent him becoming ill through infection. We also wanted him to go through his chemotherapy protocol as quickly as possible and infections would have interrupted his treatment. We believed that keeping the chemo going was our best chance to keep the tumour under control.

In hindsight, I can see that we tried to gain some control over the illness through strict adherence to the protocol. We researched the tumour and the treatment side-effects thoroughly. At times, our need to protect Owen from infections felt restrictive, but we still attended family celebrations and visited relatives, providing they were well and receiving visitors, although we asked them to wash their hands on entering our home.

The majority of our time was spent dealing with hospital appointments and hospital stays, and coping with Owen's side-effects of nausea, fatigue and various painful joints, backaches and headaches. We lived day to day with a constant fear of the next scan and the next crisis. Yet during the 16 months of Owen's chemotherapy, we still enjoyed our family life.

Everyday life for children

Play is a huge part of a child's life. Through play they explore their environment while learning skills necessary for all stages of life. Play enables a child to express emotions and feelings, and can be a useful strategy to help them come to terms with illness and express their concerns.

Young children do not have the vocabulary to explain how they feel but, through play, parents and play therapists can ascertain how they are coping. Children can explore confusing situations through play. They relate events in their life to play activities and can gain power and control through exploring issues in this way. Parents can help the child bring their experiences to their play time by play-acting hospital situations.

Playing 'clinic' was a favourite game for Owen. He enjoyed acting out the roles of phlebotomist and consultant while never wanting to play the patient. The role reversal was therapeutic for him and provided him with a sense of control over situations in which he could feel threatened or worried. In acting out the situation, he was preparing and rehearsing how he would feel and react.

It is helpful for the family to keep to a routine while allowing for flexibility during times of crisis or treatment. Routine enables everyone to have a sense of stability and security. Children with a chronic illness often feel a loss of control in their lives because of their condition, but a good routine at home helps them to feel secure.

Children respond well to consistency. They like to know the rules and boundaries. Sometimes sick children need to have more freedoms within the family. Understanding the boundaries imposed by the family is part of learning to work as a team and to be thoughtful and aware of other people. They may not always be able to do chores, complete homework or be responsible for younger siblings. However, it is important that they are encouraged to develop skills and to contribute to the family according to their age and abilities. A child's self-worth can be heightened if they feel of value in the family's daily tasks. Over-dependence on parents and siblings to carry out tasks on their behalf will inhibit their ability to cope and to develop. Parents who over-protect the sick child and prevent them from carrying out normal tasks within the family can infer that the child is too ill to contribute. A sense of inability to function normally will damage the child's self-esteem and make them over-dependent on their parents.

At the other extreme are parents who are unrealistic about the child's abilities and expect too much from them. Children who do not have a good understanding of their health problems and treatment may take risks and be too independent.

The parents should encourage the child to make decisions regarding their care and the management of their treatment and symptoms. The level of understanding of the condition and the child's ability to influence decisions is dependent on their age and development stage. The child or young person will adapt to the condition more successfully if they feel that they can have some level of impact and control over their condition. The child or young person's level of adaptation will be enhanced if they have ownership of their condition. This will allow for a more positive home and social life for the child.

Their illness or medication may make them feel angry or aggressive and they may upset siblings with their behaviour. While this is not acceptable, the child needs to feel understanding and support. Parents can explain why the child's behaviour is not acceptable and impose appropriate discipline within reason.

Long-term management of a chronic condition can be tiresome for both a parent and the child, and can cause children to be resentful. One mother explained the daily demands of caring for her son's eczema:

> Our day begins with the same routine. In the morning Matthew's skin is often raw and bleeding where he has managed to tear at it in the night. I bathe him in special bath oil and apply his creams. His creams are applied at least three times a day, all over. The creams sting him and he becomes distressed. He becomes upset and I become stressed trying to comfort him while still needing to apply the cream. When the eczema is particularly bad he has to be creamed and then wrapped in gauze and bandages to stop him scratching at his skin. I try to get him to sleep with mittens on but he finds them uncomfortable.

While this child with eczema resented his regular applications of creams and bandages, his mother tried to convey a sense of working together to deal with his condition.

The parents' first concern is securing good healthcare and support to enable them to cope with the difficult circumstances presented by chronic illness. While every child's condition brings unique problems and demands, all families coping with chronic illness face similar challenges in dealing with medics, teachers, well siblings and general everyday life.

Two of the main concerns facing all parents are about nutrition and sleep patterns. Children with a chronic illness can develop sleep disturbance patterns because of their illness. Chronic pain, side-effects of medication, symptoms or repeated hospital stays can all have an impact on the child's sleep patterns.

Parents often find that they too can experience sleep problems, related to the ongoing disruption to their sleep when they need to attend to the child. Some children with a chronic illness are dependent on technology, such as a ventilator, which has implications for sleep. Parents often have to check on the child, adjust equipment or even try sleeping with the constant hum of the machinery.

While sleep disruption is physically and mentally draining for parents and the child, it can be difficult to impose a routine when treatment, hospital stays and periods of illness regularly cause ongoing disruption. Nevertheless, a regular night-time routine is important and can help establish better sleep patterns, if not solve the sleep problems all together.

Conditions such as psoriasis and eczema can cause sleep disruption because the skin can become itchy and inflamed during the night. One child living with severe eczema experienced episodes of intense itchiness during the night. His mother described how she would attend to him:

> He would be very itchy during the night and would move around the bed to rub his feet and arms and back on the mattress to ease the itch. I often end up rubbing his back and gently scratching his back and ankles until he is asleep again.

Some children with juvenile arthritis or cerebral palsy need to be turned in their sleep, and the parent must wake during the night to adjust the child's position.

Children who do not have to adhere to bedtime routines develop sleep problems. They do not know how to wind down and relax prior to bedtime. It can be difficult to establish a good bedtime routine if the child is spending a lot of time in hospital. Hospitals at night time are not always quiet. Nurses continue the business of monitoring the child; lights dimmed but still on, the whirr of the IV pumps and other hospital equipment, and the need to wake a child to give them medication all affect the child's sleep pattern. Parents find that their need to be vigilant, listening out for a sick child during the night, can prevent them from achieving deep sleep.

It can be difficult to enforce regular routines for bedtime with a sick child. When parents aim to create a family routine that involves discipline and respect, they are helping to normalize the child's condition. If the child is treated differently in every aspect of their lives, they will feel different and isolated. Parents who do not set boundaries are preventing their child from being well adjusted and able to cope with their condition. A child who dictates when they go to bed will not have enough rest and will feel tired the next day. Their symptoms and pain will also be more difficult to manage if they are fatigued.

Ensuring that a child with a chronic illness receives adequate nutrition can be a source of stress for parents. Children can find that food is one of the few areas of their lives where they can gain control. Many parents have described how food becomes a battle. They want their child to eat a healthy diet. When a child is chronically ill, good nutrition becomes even more important in the parents' mind and so the responsibility to ensure that the child eats, and eats healthily, becomes a source of stress.

Some conditions such as diabetes, coeliac disease and peanut allergy are largely concerned with controlling food and managing the child's diet. The child can use food as an act of defiance and rebellion. They can feel isolated within the family if their diet is restricted. If it is possible, parents should try to provide the same meal for the whole family to avoid the child's sense of isolation. Likewise, if a child finds the family meal unappetizing due to their treatment, as in the case of chemotherapy, then it is difficult to expect the well siblings to eat what they are given without choice. Adapting the family's diet to suit the needs of the child may seem extreme and unfair but, with some creativity and research, parents can incorporate the child's food needs into the family menus.

Sometimes children who are not able to eat well are told by their medics to eat anything, even unhealthy foods, to help their calorie intake. Children with cystic fibrosis generally need a greater calorie intake than their peers. To ensure that such a child is maintaining a good calorie intake with the required supplements, the parents and the child need to work with a dietician to create meal plans. Similarly, some children with pancreatic insufficiency are required to take enzymes with their meals to help with digestion.

One parent spoke of her frustrations in trying to make her son eat healthy food while he was being treated for leukaemia:

> Meal times were an ordeal. I would cook one meal and he would ask for something different. I would try to cook healthy dinners but all he wanted was junk food. In the end I would just give him whatever he wanted.

When the child was being treated with steroids, she described how he was constantly hungry: 'We went from one extreme to another. I couldn't give him enough food to satisfy him.'

Food issues can cause feelings of inadequacy and failure in parents. The most conscientious and attentive parent can occasionally make mistakes when it comes to the child's diet. A child with allergies can be at risk from a variety of foods and, while parents are vigilant, it can be difficult to monitor their food intake at all times. If a child has to be tube-fed, mothers in particular feel that they have failed to nurture their child. One mother described how she felt about tube-feeding:

> The feeding tube signified that I couldn't look after my son, that I couldn't carry out my role as a mother. While I knew it was to help him I still felt guilty.

> I also resented that the tube stayed in all day. When we were out people would notice the feeding tube and see that he was ill. It was like a stigma.

During Owen's chemotherapy, eating was difficult for him. Bland, simple foods like bananas and bread and butter were his staples along with milk. As a mother, it was painful to watch him lose weight and struggle to eat. He never sat at the table with the rest of the family during meal times because the smell of our food would make him retch. He gained no pleasure from eating and, although he would sometimes eat a cookie or some chocolate, on the whole he never ate sweets. He did enjoy McDonald's fries though, and we became regular customers.

When his chemotherapy treatment ended, I struggled to improve Owen's diet. He and I shopped together and cooked together as I tried to be creative in motivating him to try new foods. I was desperate to create appetizing meals for him. At one stage, I consulted a child psychologist to discuss Owen's food issues. I dreaded going, assuming that she would insist that his poor diet was a result of over-indulgence during his chemotherapy and that he had learned bad eating habits that I would need to change. Instead, she listened while I recounted Owen's fussy eating as a toddler, while I explained that during chemo he suffered extreme nausea, that he had developed a peanut allergy at the age of four and that I had tried every star chart motivational technique imaginable but still he could not manage to eat a proper family meal. At the end of listening to me, she simply said I had tried everything she could have suggested and that, if he was growing and putting some of the weight that he had lost during his chemo back on, then to try to just go with his food choices. It was such a huge relief for someone to tell me it was okay for Owen not to be eating healthy food. I felt vindicated in my belief that somehow his tumour had affected his sense of taste and that neither Owen nor I could repair his lack of interest in eating. While I continued to introduce new foods to Owen and tried to create nutritious and appetizing meals for him, at least I did so without feeling a failure every time the meal went uneaten.

It is tempting for parents to over-indulge children with a chronic illness, trying to compensate for their suffering or lack of ability. But what all children want is normality and for their parents to parent them well. A parent who spoils or over-indulges a sick child is giving them negative messages – that is, that they need to have more to make up for deficiencies created by their illness. A cycle of expectation is created and the child becomes demanding and less likeable. A chronically sick child will find it more difficult to interact with peers and siblings if they expect to be treated advantageously. The sister of a child diagnosed with a terminal cancer described how she felt about her brother receiving presents from relatives on a regular basis:

> It felt unfair that he would get gifts more or less every day. I knew he needed them to try to make his life more bearable and to stop him being bored but I just felt left out.

> I told my counsellor how I felt and she explained that my aunts and uncles couldn't help my brother so they try to make up for his sickness by buying him stuff. That helped me to understand that it wasn't about leaving me out but rather helping my brother cope with his disease.

Other people, family members, friends and teachers will not be so tolerant and the child may have to struggle to adjust to the difference in how others treat them.

Parents may feel that they do not spoil a child because they do not over-indulge them with toys or treats. However, how they *treat* the child can be part of the problem. Parents often struggle to set limits and fail to create fairness between siblings. While this is a disservice to the well children, it also has a negative impact on the ill child. For a child to develop into a well-adjusted adult, they need to understand compromise and respect. When parents fail to create a structured routine with boundaries for the family to grow and show mutual respect and love, they are indirectly telling the child that they are not in control.

One parent of a child diagnosed with cerebral palsy said, 'I never wanted to spoil him. I would be doing the child a disservice to spoil him. Maybe you give them more hugs and kisses but the boundaries should remain.'

A child living with a chronic condition experiences a loss of control; they are undergoing treatment which limits their activities and abilities. If the parents appear not to be in control of family life, then the child can become anxious and insecure. A parent's lack of control can relate to simple everyday routines such as no set bed times and permission to watch television or eat unhealthy foods whenever the child wants. One mother told me how she was determined to treat her son normally because she didn't want to 'pity him'. She realized that, in trying to continue her parenting as normally as his illness allowed, she was giving him the normality he wanted.

While I write this and fully appreciate the theory behind not over-indulging a sick child, I can also admit that the reality is often different. Owen had every video-gaming console and PlayStation game imaginable. He was frequently bought toys and books by us and family members. But, when you consider how often he had to stay in hospital receiving chemotherapy and then enduring the side-effects when he was at home, it is understandable that we tried to alleviate his boredom and offer him distractions from the nausea and pain.

Many sick children become experts in computer gaming and parents often feel guilty that their child spends so much time in front of a computer or television. Research has shown that video games can help children cope with pain and nausea. Hospital-based Online Pediatric Environment (HOPE) provides children with a chronic illness with the distraction of gaming to help them endure their symptoms. HOPE believes that, through peer contact in a virtual world of gaming, children will be better able to reduce perceived pain and prevent depression, thus improving the quality of life.

Dr Arun Mathews, who works with HOPE, identified video gaming as being a useful mechanism whereby children and parents could interact during hospital stays:

> I recall a story about a sick child on chemotherapy whose father would travel quite a bit. They would however agree to meet up online and play the dungeon adventure game *Diablo*, and this seemed to do wonders in terms of alleviating the child's sense of isolation.
>
> As the child was clearly better [at playing the game] there was a wonderful role-reversal that took place, with the child actively having to 'protect' his lesser adept father from the attacks of the demon horde.

Children undergoing dialysis can be hooked up to a dialysis machine three times a week for at least three hours at a time. Access to video games for these children can help them cope with the enforced periods of inactivity and boredom.

Video gaming allowed Owen to compete with his peers on an equal level. While he didn't always have the energy and stamina to play football, he could play video games until near the end of his life. His self-esteem was greatly enhanced through his ability to achieve high scores and compete equally with his friends. Video gaming improved his mental arithmetic along with his ability to solve puzzles and think logically.

While no parent would advocate video gaming 12 hours a day, it can play a huge part in helping children with a chronic illness cope with their illness if it is used in conjunction with other forms of play and activities. As Dr Mathews explains:

> The fact remains that gaming itself is a type of education, albeit a highly abstract, extremely compelling one. It demands interaction, and in this sense is diametrically opposed to the unidirectional flow of information in a film or on a TV show.
>
> Whether stiffening up the suspension of a Japanese touring car, or flying in between two binary stars, the point is that these games can at the very least distract a child from agonizing circumstances, and, at the most, broaden a child's mind with experiences he or she may never be able to experience in reality.

Children living with chronic illness often experience low self-esteem. Limitations imposed by their condition and the side-effects of their treatment create a sense of being less able than their peers. They are treated as being different by their peers and find that even if they strive for normality there will be periods when they cannot participate in everyday activities. Dr Mathews believes that:

> Children coping with chronic illness are heroes. Of this, there is no question. Unfortunately, sometimes they don't realize this. Gaming empowers children, allowing them to inhabit, in the virtual realm, bodies and health denied to them 'offline' by way of illness. Let them be leaders of armies, sports heroes, and secret agents.

Families with children who are dependent on medical technology such as ventilators can face great difficulty in trying to normalize their lives and create a life outside the home. All children desire to be like their siblings and peers. It is important to try not to allow the child's condition to define them. If it is possible, families should schedule time to deal with medical demands, order prescriptions on a certain day of the week, check medical equipment and make follow-up appointments. If these ongoing demands on the family time can be limited to a certain day, then the family will feel less dominated by the condition.

Regular outings and physical activity can help ease stress. Families who spend a lot of time in hospital would benefit from scheduling time to engage in exercise and sport as a stress reliever. While this is not always possible, even a short walk around the hospital grounds can help.

Everyday life for teenagers

The adolescent years are challenging for everyone but for those living with a chronic condition the problems are confounded. Identity, self-image, establishing independence, peer pressure and acceptance, and sexuality are all normal teenage concerns. For the teenager with a chronic illness, these issues are further complicated by the restrictions of their condition and treatment. They can be frustrated by their lack of control and independence, and feel alienated from their peers. As they struggle to assert their independence from their parents, they find that during periods of illness or treatment their dependence on their parents is heightened.

The need for independence and the struggle against the limitations of the condition can bring about low self-esteem and even depression.[6] Teenagers with a chronic illness can feel self-conscious about their condition. Most adolescents experience self-doubt and insecurities. It is a period of intense growth and change, physically and emotionally. The concerns that most adolescents experience are further complicated by the chronic condition. Limitations imposed by the illness, changes to the appearance, repeated hospitalizations and treatment protocols can all adversely affect the adolescent's sense of psychological wellbeing.

The young person can be resentful that they are limited by their illness, and react by refusing to comply with treatment. Non-compliance may not be direct or aggressive but instead a gradual reluctance to be mindful of their condition. For instance, when a young person is socializing with their friends, they will not want to draw attention to their illness by taking medication or making choices regarding their diet. For example, a young person with diabetes may find it difficult to monitor their diet while in the company of friends.

If a young person is displaying a pattern of refusing to comply with treatment, they should be encouraged to talk about their feelings and explore ways in which they can be more positive about the management of their condition. Sometimes it is necessary for the adolescent to speak with their healthcare professionals to discuss their treatment and to develop a full understanding of the impact of their non-compliance. It is important for the young person to be actively involved in designing their care plans. Health professionals need to have an understanding of the young person's life in order to adjust the treatment if at all possible to be more easily managed.

Chronic illness can have an impact on the teenager's confidence and self-esteem. The condition can be affected by the increased growth and development of the adolescent, sometimes exacerbating symptoms. Chronic illness can bring about changes to the appearance and affect the young person's self-confidence. Parents can discuss these with the medics and the young person. It is important to ascertain if the changes will be permanent or diminish once symptoms disappear or medication ends. The psychological impact of physical changes can be significant and, if the young person does not adapt to them, they can become withdrawn and depressed. Self-esteem is often dependent on self-image. The teenager should be encouraged to talk about their self-image and how they feel about the changes. If the changes are permanent, then it is worth examining the positive aspects of the young person's life and trying to help them put the physical changes into perspective. If the changes are caused by treatment such as hair loss as a result of chemotherapy, then the young person should be encouraged to view the temporary hair loss as a trade-off to overcoming the cancer.

While freedoms and independence are often curtailed by illness, the adolescent will cope better if they are kept fully informed about their health condition and feel like an active participant in decisions regarding their healthcare rather than a patient with no control or voice. The personal strengths and abilities of the young person should be recognized and utilized by the health professionals. If the young person feels confident in communicating to their parents and their health professionals, they will be more able to express their needs. If their needs are addressed, the young person will be more competent in managing their care and will develop a more positive approach to the integration of their illness into their everyday life.

The adolescent should have privacy and space. Parents can overprotect and invade the young person's privacy by feeling that they need to be with them at all times. The dressing and washing of a young person who is physically limited and dependent on help needs to be reassessed during the adolescent years. Sometimes the young person may want to attend hospital appointments alone or have the opportunity to talk to their medics without their parents present. While they can feel vulnerable and helpless during particular periods of their illness, they also struggle to balance this with their need to be assertive and independent.

Adolescence is a period of adjustment for the parent–child relationship. This is complicated by chronic illness in that the sense of dependency may be increased rather than decreased. Parents should try to foster flexibility when imposing rules and boundaries. During periods of wellness, the young person's ability to socialize and enjoy freedoms can be increased while it may need to be curtailed during periods of crisis or treatment. The parents need to work with the young person to balance the need for independence and individuality with their need to protect and provide boundaries. Friendships are important to the adolescent's emotional development. To develop a healthy self-image and identity, the young person with a chronic illness must be able to develop relationships with their peers and feel accepted by them. The social life of a young person can be a positive coping strategy that allows for emotional support and enhanced self-esteem.

Many children with a chronic illness experience growth problems and delayed puberty. An adolescent with cystic fibrosis can have delayed puberty and small stature, which can present problems with confidence and self-esteem. Children and young people with brain tumours are sometimes treated with steroids that cause weight gain and fluid retention. The changes to appearance can be difficult for the child to adjust to. Changes to physical appearance can also be caused by radical surgery resulting in disfigurement, scarring or loss of a limb. If changes to appearance caused by the chronic condition or treatment can be anticipated, then it is better to discuss the changes and how they will affect the young person.

The close relationship between parents and the young person with a chronic illness can cause parents to believe that their child is not in need of the same advice and information about sexual behaviour as other teenagers. Adolescents with a chronic illness have the same need for information about their body as other young people. Sex education may be overlooked because of developmental delays but parents should be aware of the need to prepare the young person for adulthood. The young person deserves to have clear, accurate information about sex and how their condition affects their sexual development and their fertility. Health professionals can guide parents and the young person on matters of sex education and sexual maturity. The adolescent with a chronic illness is still a teenager with the same concerns and doubts as any other teenager.

Adolescence is a period during which young people begin to assert their independence from their parents – they change schools, make new friends, develop new relationships and interests, undertake exams and begin working towards their future career aspirations. Chronic illness can affect the adolescent in all these areas.

Educational attainment is a huge factor in the adolescent's life. They make choices about subjects they wish to study, which can have an impact on their long-term career aspirations. They should be encouraged to maintain their goals and ambitions while making decisions according to their needs and abilities. The young person may strive to perform well academically and hope to pursue further studies, while another young person may choose a more vocational career path and explore ways in which to realize their ambitions. Planning for the future and maintaining ambitions is a coping strategy. Promoting a positive outlook for the future can enhance the young person's self-esteem and help them to focus on fulfilling their aspirations rather than feeling limited by their condition.

The adolescent with a chronic illness must also deal with the transition from paediatric care to adult care. In some instances, the transition occurs at 16 years of age and in other hospitals it is at 18. Parents need to be mindful of the effect of the handover period on the young person. They can feel a sense of abandonment moving from health professionals they know well to a new environment with medics who are used to dealing with adult patients. Careful planning and collaboration is required to ensure a smooth transition.

❖ Advice and action points ❖

- *Create* a family mission statement. Think about what is important to your family and work at how to achieve it.

- *Develop* goals to help achieve some time outside the demands of the family to recharge and re-energize.

- *Live* in the present and enjoy today.

- *Respect* each other and be mindful of allowing stress and anger to be directed at family members.

- *Maintain* structure, routine and organization, but allow for flexibility during periods of crisis.

- *Remember* that discipline and punishment are different. Good parenting is about disciplining with encouragement and supporting the child to understand that good behaviour is rewarded with praise. Consistency creates stability and security.

- *Accept* invitations. Although outings, celebrations and holidays may be challenging, with good preparation and planning they are achievable and worthwhile.

- *Evaluate* how all family members are coping on an ongoing basis. The impact of the chronic condition can be variable and parents need to be aware of how the whole family is affected.

- *Incorporate* the illness into family life. Accept that there will be changes and adjustments, and work around them to achieve a new normality.

- *Identify* barriers to creating a social life, and work to overcome them.

- *Be organized* and if possible try to limit the amount of time spent in hospital by scheduling appointments for one day. Develop a routine for ordering medicines and administering them. This will help to minimize the impact of the treatment on family life.

- *Encourage* individual family members to engage in activities outside the family, thereby creating a network of support.

- *Keep talking* and *listening* to each other. Ongoing family communication will increase a sense of togetherness and help strengthen the family bond.

The challenges of integrating chronic illness into everyday family life can be met through adapting and re-organization. Part of learning to manage the condition is to achieve a sense of normality and to cope with the demands of family life while living with the chronic illness. Be gentle with yourself and take care of each other.

7

When Hope Fades: Parenting a Child who is Terminally Ill

Developments in medicine have improved the survival rate of many illnesses that would previously have caused death in infancy or early childhood. Many children and young people have their lives prolonged through surgery, treatment and medical intervention.

In some chronic conditions, premature death does occur. The threat of a chronic condition becoming terminal can cause stress and impede a parent's ability to cope. They live with a constant fear of the condition becoming worse and are watchful for symptoms that may suggest progression. Families of children who have a terminal condition experience prolonged and unrelenting anxiety and stress. While they live with the pain of knowing their child is dying, they try to carry out normal everyday tasks, caring for the child's medical needs without breaking down. They often experience anticipatory grief, living through the pain of knowing their child will die. The challenge of parenting a dying child is in ensuring that they are not distressed by the parents' trauma and that their quality of life is as good as possible.

Differing factors influence the dying process and how the child and the family cope. How old is the child? What is their developmental understanding of death? Are they at home or in hospital or a hospice setting? Are they comfortable and pain-free? Are the other family members able to participate in the child's final weeks or days?

The dying process is an individual one, and how the family copes can have an impact on the child's wellbeing. Parenting a dying child is parenting in the extreme. Emotions are heightened and stress levels appear unbearable. There is little research into how families cope at this time. The level of care required to look after the dying child, coupled with the intense emotional strain on parents, means that few families would want to participate in research. Parents need to try to protect the child from their trauma and emotional distress.

A parent who has to live with the knowledge that their child is dying can find their previous coping ability to be suddenly fragile.[1] The demands of caring for a child with a chronic illness, compounded with the reality of losing them, can create stress and pre-empt the grieving process.

Parents can experience a feeling of intense loneliness when caring for a dying child. For one mother, caring for her ten-year-old dying son was one such isolating experience:

> Really and truly whenever I went through this period I felt very isolated. Both my parents were dead and my siblings worked and had their own lives so I spent every day on my own with the child. He did not like to leave the house so apart from my Crossroads lady and the hospice nurse I felt very isolated. My child got so ill that he just wanted quiet time.

Once a terminal diagnosis has been made, the focus of medical intervention and treatment becomes about controlling symptoms and trying to ensure that the child has a good quality of life if at all possible.[2] The parents' ability to cope at this difficult time is central in helping the child to live the remainder of their life in comfort while still having some enjoyment. The aim is to live well and live fully within the limits of the condition.

Some families can find comfort and solace in their religious or spiritual beliefs. Their strength and coping ability lie in the belief that the family will be reunited one day. One mother described how she relied on her faith to try to understand her child's condition: 'Religion was my coping strategy. I tried to make sense of this life. Praying for a miracle trying to believe that there was a reason for this…to try and make sense of it all.'

Others find that the constant demands and the sense of crisis and urgency keep them focused and assist their coping ability. They try to stay in control of events through being active and responsive to the child's needs. The emotional trauma of watching a child die cannot be under-estimated, but the ability to be resilient and maintain a sense of control over the emotional distress is often the consequence of a parent trying to do their best for their child. The acute grief gives way to an underlying sadness, but at times the intense pain of losing a child does seem uncontrollable. No one can maintain the high anxiety levels of the initial trauma. There is a sense of shutting down, functioning with a numbness or a sense of removal from the situation. Emotions and anxieties peak periodically and become heightened at times often related to crisis points, the onset of respiratory difficulty, increased pain levels, infections and loss of control of the limbs or bowels – whatever the progression of the condition entails.

The final days and weeks of a child's life, and how a child dies, can have a huge impact on how the family copes with their bereavement. The pain and suffering of a dying child can cause long-term depression in parents. Parents can experience extreme stress as they care for their dying child. They may be faced with decisions regarding stopping aggressive medical treatment. Some parents feel obliged to continue treatment, fearing that in not treating the child they are surrendering and giving up. Decisions regarding end of life treatment should be made with the advice of the medical team. Parents need to feel satisfied that they have explored all options and that it is in the child's best interests to move to palliative care.

Parents also make choices regarding end of life care and treatment to manage symptoms. They must also decide how to communicate with their child at the end stage of their life, as well as considering the impact on the well siblings and how to facilitate their coping.

Health professionals are in the business of curing. End of life issues can be difficult for medics to deal with especially when the patient is a child. How the health professionals communicate to the parents at such a difficult time can have an impact on the parents' coping ability. Parents need information delivered in a caring and sensitive way. They need to be kept fully informed and supported in making decisions.

Palliative care is about meeting the physical and spiritual needs of a child when all hope of cure has gone. The focus should be on making the child comfortable, pain-free and content. The move to palliative care can be difficult for parents to accept. However, in addressing the end of life needs of the child, rather than continuing aggressive treatment that holds no hope, the parents are providing the child with exceptional parenting. Palliative care is supportive care, which aims to manage the child's death in a dignified and caring manner.[3] Compassion, understanding, sensitivity and emotional support are required to help families cope and, in assisting the family to maintain their ability to look after the child, the health professionals are having a direct influence on the child's quality of life.

When we think of palliative care, we think of quality of life. Ensuring that the child is comfortable is a priority. It is also important to provide the child with a sense of normality. They want to continue normal activities if at all possible. They will want contact with friends, to play video games, read, paint, whatever it is that makes them happy. Knowing that the child is dying can place a huge burden on the parents; while they want to behave and function normally, they find themselves in the most abnormal situation. The emotional trauma of parenting a dying child can place a huge psychological burden on the parents. They feel responsible for ensuring that their child is not in pain or discomfort. They want to provide their child with love, security and contentment while they themselves are falling apart and feeling vulnerable.

Many parents describe how their child's resilience and coping ability helps them. One father described his dying son's ability to cope and how it had an impact on how the family coped: 'He carried us all. How could we not cope when he was still wanting to live and worried about us?' Many children display great depths of feeling and leave a legacy of love. Owen certainly made sure that those he was closest to knew how much he loved them. He also continued caring for us even while he was suffering extreme pain. He would worry about his sister and ask who was picking her up from school.

One mother caring for her dying son described it as a 'deep privilege'. She felt that she had gained a special closeness to her son:

> You reach levels in your parenting that you wouldn't reach if it wasn't for that situation. Most parents never get there. It was almost this telepathic communication; I just needed to look at him to

know what he needed and he knew when he needed to rally to give me something back.

Parents can be comforted in knowing that they were resilient and strong for the child in death – that they coped and did not cause the child distress by being overcome by anxiety and devastation in front of them. Family life must continue to function if the child is to have some sense of normality and be content during the remainder of their life. This is especially important for the child dying at home. The sense of 'allowing' a child to die because they have endured much suffering is a recurring theme for parents who have cared for children with degenerative conditions. One mother explained her feeling of accepting her son's imminent death:

> The turning point for me was the day I promised him I would not spoil one day of his time by moaning and crying. I can live with his death because I knew he had suffered enough and we as a family had done everything in our power to make him as comfortable and happy as possible. So therefore you must 'enjoy' the time you have and at the end I was on my knees praying to God to take him as I could not bear to see him suffer any more. My child was skin and bones at the time of his death. It was time for his death. He just was not meant for this world any longer.

> He was loved very much and gave us so much love that I would not have swapped him for the world. It was a privilege to have had him and care for him. I can look back at extremely funny things he did and the laughter he had in his own special world.

Decisions regarding where the child should spend the last weeks or days of their life can be difficult for some families. Not all families can accommodate the child at home. Factors concerning siblings, medication and pain management may dictate that the child's welfare is better served in a hospital or hospice environment. If the child is dependent on medical technology, hospital is sometimes the only option. Some families with younger children feel that they prefer to care for their dying child at hospital or in a hospice so that they can give them their undivided attention. Parents must do what feels right for their child and them.

For us it was imperative that Owen died at home. He had spent enough time in hospital and, as long as we knew he was receiving all the relevant medication at home, we were determined that he should be able to be surrounded by family at home for the remainder of his life.

Support from close family and community medics is vital to assist the child dying at home. We were well supported by our community practitioners. The community nurses worked alongside our general practitioners and the local pharmacist to assist us. We had help around the house and Carol, our family support worker who spent time with Kate, also helped with household chores. The community play therapist, Naomi, whom Owen loved, spent some time with him doing creative activities and his teacher, Margaret, read to him. We also had telephone contact with Owen's consultant oncologist who still maintained an active interest in Owen's care. In short, we had a team of people along with our extended family, supporting us and helping Owen.

For the child to stay at home, many people need to be involved. Some families resent the intrusion at such a traumatic time in their lives. They want to care for their child without interference from health professionals or family members. In most cases, to provide the quality of care the child needs, support is essential. The support available to the family needs to include a core group of health professionals. Parents should not have to deal with numerous medics or agencies in negotiating their child's care.

It is also preferable to have continuity of care. The child and the parents should not be 'handed' over to a new set of health professionals at such a stressful time. Sometimes specialist equipment is needed – hoists, beds, special mattresses, mobility aids, sensory equipment. Parents need to be able to access such equipment without delays.

The emotional and physical drain of caring for a child who is terminally ill can be wearing. To enable the parents to provide the child with such care requires additional support. Other family members need to be looked after. The household tasks need to be completed and the endless phone calls and visitors need to be attended to. Family and close friends can be valuable in helping with these tasks.

If towards the end of life the health professionals who had been actively treating the child no longer have contact with the family, there can be a sense of abandonment and isolation. Some families feel that their doctors send their child home to die and do not offer guidance and support when they need it most. Families need to feel that the loss of their child is significant to all those who have been active in their care management.

The focus of the child's care moves from being curative to managing symptoms and enhancing quality of life. It can be difficult for parents to move from a seemingly curative treatment plan to a palliative one. Even though chronic illnesses are not curable, parents can resist acknowledging the possibility of premature death. When there is a resistance to accepting palliative care, the child's wellbeing can be compromised in that it may be more difficult to ensure a peaceful death.

If parents are able to plan and prepare for end of life care, then they are more likely to be able to access services and care to support their child.[4] Discussing end of life issues such as resuscitation, the use of opiates, where the child should die and other dilemmas in advance can help parents to be prepared and deal with the issues as they arise.

Despite improvements in pain management, some children still die in pain. Inadequate pain management can be due to several factors: pain in children can be under-estimated and medics can be reluctant to prescribe opiates; there can be a fear of over-prescribing opiates and overdosing children, and children can be limited in communicating their pain; and sometimes the side-effects of the pain medication interfere with the child's wellbeing. Although Owen's pain was managed as well as possible, he still suffered immensely. The side-effects of opiates include constipation, nausea, itching, drowsiness and respiratory problems. Often the side-effects of pain management can cause great discomfort. Pamela Surkan, research fellow at the Harvard School of Public Health, has examined the differences in the pain of children dying at home compared to hospital environments: 'Our study found no differences in relief of pain or other kinds of care for children dying of a malignancy at home versus in a hospital facility.' The study conducted in Sweden also found:

> Home care appeared to be equivalent to hospital care in terms of satisfactory pain-relief as well as access to relief of other physical and psychological symptoms.

> End-of-life home care was comparable to hospital care for satisfactory pain relief, access to pain relief and access to medications for other physical symptoms.[5]

It is often possible for health professionals to anticipate symptoms in advance. They should prepare the parents and explain the possible outcomes and how they hope to deal with the symptoms as they arise. The medics and the parents should discuss how the pain relief is to be administered and be prepared for the use of long-term venous access devices. The child should be closely monitored and assessed to ensure the effectiveness of their pain management.

When a child is terminally ill, treatment and management of symptoms should be instant. If preparation and discussion has taken place prior to symptoms worsening, then the medics can react quickly. A written plan, detailing whom to call and which drugs to be administered, can help parents to feel prepared and more in control. When several drugs are being administered in the home, it is useful for the parents to have a timetable drawn up to ensure that the correct doses are given over the 24-hour period.

Parents can offer the child distraction from their pain or discomfort by reading to them, playing music, video games or guided imagery. It is important to reassure the child, even when they are heavily sedated or unconscious.

Talking about death

All children have some concept of death. They may have experience of losing a grandparent, a friend or family pet, or they may have derived their idea of death from a religious upbringing. Children see images of death on television, in video games and in books. The child's age, development stage and emotional maturity will all affect how they view death.[6]

The child with a chronic illness is often significantly aware of their condition and it can be difficult to exclude them from knowledge of their impending death if this is the parents' preferred option. These children and young people have invested time in learning about their condition; they are aware of their limitations and knowledgeable about their treatment. They are also susceptible to the emotions of those around them and can be apt at reading their parents and the medics. They can also have a greater understanding of the fragility of life than most of their peers.

Many parents struggle with the child's right to know issue. For some families, telling the child about their anticipated death is simply too painful. They cannot cope with the idea of their child being fearful of death. Children with a chronic illness are often described as being resilient. Their life experiences are different from those of their peers and often they possess a heightened sense of empathy and idealism as a result. While it is wrong to destroy hope for the future, it is also wrong to predict death. A child will ask questions, sometimes direct ones about their death. In response to such questions, parents should be encouraged to be truthful while allowing the child to draw the conclusions that suit them. For instance, if a child asks directly 'Am I going to die?', the parent can reply, 'Well, we are all going to die some day.' If the child is not satisfied with this answer and wants to be more specific, the parent can ask them, 'What do you think about death?' The parent can explain that the medics are doing all they can to prolong the child's life. A discussion about what the child thinks occurs after death can be reassuring for a child. If they have their own ideas of what heaven is like, they should be allowed to talk about it.

In discussing death, the parent wants to reassure the child rather than cause them increased anxiety. It can be difficult for the parents not to anticipate death and enter a period of premature mourning. However, allowing oneself to explore such powerful emotions while the child is still alive can have an impact on one's coping ability. The needs of the child are paramount and if at all possible the parent should try to stay focused on the child and keep their own anxieties under control. It is challenging to maintain a sense of normality and to care for the dying child without breaking down. A sense of despair and desolation can engulf families and add to the child's own sense of fear and sadness.

In one study, researchers sought to establish how parents felt about their conversations with their dying child: did parents of children who had died from cancer regret not having talked about death or, if they did talk about it, did they wish they hadn't?

> Parents who sense that their child is aware of his or her imminent death more often later regret not having talked with their child than do parents who do not sense this awareness in their child; overall, no parent in this cohort later regretted having talked with his or her child about death.[7]

One mother told me how she discussed death with her six-year-old daughter:

> She used to ask, 'When am I going to get better?' And in the beginning I would have talked about getting better for Christmas and distracted her with talk about other things, but then she asked me if she was going to die and I said, 'Yes, I am going to die, Daddy is going to die, everyone is going to die.' She assumed when I said everyone that she too was going to die but in chronological order.
>
> I focused on heaven and told her there was nothing to be afraid of, and religion really helped me to explain death to her and that time doesn't make any difference in heaven. Religion helped me to explain to her that age and time means nothing and we would be reunited again as a family.
>
> I don't regret talking to her about death. I feel it was right to discuss such a difficult thing with her. I talked to her in terms she could relate to and cope with.

Research has shown that children, even very young children, have an awareness of their imminent death. However, parents may want to try to protect the child from knowing that they are dying.[8] The age and development of the child, along with religious and cultural traditions, are all relevant to how much information they should be given.

To avoid discussing death with a child can increase their sense of isolation and fear. Often the child and the parent respond to each other with mutual denial, each trying to protect the other.

Treating death as part of the life cycle can help the child to eliminate their fears and anxieties. While a child may have no knowledge of their imminent death, they can be susceptible to the fears and anxieties of their parents and siblings. It can be difficult for the parents to protect them from those around them and how they react to the child.

How we prepare for and respond to death differs according to our spiritual and cultural backgrounds. Some families utilize religion as a coping mechanism. They can feel comforted believing that there is an afterlife and that their separation will be temporary.[9]

A change in the child's behaviour often indicates that they are worried or frightened. Young children often speak about their fears of others dying. They experience separation anxiety and are fretful about being alone.

Some children can find it difficult to communicate their fears and can become aggressive and over-emotional. Another child may become withdrawn and quiet. If the parents feel that the child may need to talk about their worries, they can instigate discussion with open questions. The parent can begin by encouraging the child to talk about how they feel. They can ask how they can help the child. Often sharing fears and concerns helps to alleviate some of the anxiety.

Some adolescents display their anxiety through being regressive and withdrawn. Others can become aggressive and refuse to comply with treatment in their desperation to assert control.

If parents are worried about the child's emotional wellbeing, they can discuss their concerns with their health professionals. It is sometimes worth speaking to a psychologist. Young children in particular find it difficult to understand the permanence and irreversibility of death. Hospice nurses are experienced in caring for the dying and can help alleviate fears in the whole family.

One care worker who has helped families during their child's final weeks said, 'If possible, the best way for a child to die is at home, surrounded by family.' She believes that siblings cope better if they are included in the child's final days. Siblings can be overlooked in the need for communication about death. The need for care and attention can be focused solely on the dying child and siblings can feel excluded. They can be aware of their dying brother or sister but feel unable to communicate their fears and worries. They may wish to spend time with their sibling but be kept away from them.

As the illness progresses and worsens, the child's sense of fear and anxiety may be heightened. They are aware of the emotions of those around them and are apt at reading their parents' thoughts. Parents should respond to their fears by being empathetic and supportive rather than dismissive. It is tempting to tell a child that everything will be all right, but this often only serves the parent's desire to not address the child's fears directly. It is better to acknowledge the child's worries, and tell them that you understand and that you too are worried. Offer comfort in explaining that the medics are looking after the child's needs and that you will be close by at all times.

Adolescents may be able to communicate their anxieties but choose to do so with someone other than their parents. They need to be listened to without feeling responsible for upsetting those closest to them. Parents need to ensure that the young person has a sense of independence if possible, and that they have privacy and dignity. Ongoing communication and contact with their friends should be encouraged.

❖ Advice and action points ❖

- *Establish* a core support group dedicated to supporting your child at the end of life, and be clear what you expect them to offer your child.

- *Communicate* with your child at their level. Address their concerns and questions with openness and honesty appropriate for their age and development.

- *Encourage* your child to express their fears and worries by being open and initiating discussions.

- *Demand* pain control. Research pain management options and be assertive in demanding swift action from medics.

- *Evaluate* the care plan and pain management on an ongoing basis. Assess your child's quality of life and determine how to improve it.

- *Involve* siblings. Research has shown that siblings who are excluded at the end of the child's life do not cope with their grief as well as those who feel involved.

- *Be clear* about your expectations and fears. Discuss with the core support group how you anticipate the death to be, what pain management options are available, where you want the child to be cared for and how much intervention you want from medics. The death of a child is a traumatic event. Be gentle with yourself and those close to you.

Conclusion

Children living with chronic illness deserve the best possible treatment. They should be encouraged to live a full life, striving to be independent according to their abilities.

Caring for children with a chronic illness is a privilege. These children experience so much adversity in their lives but show great resilience and strength of character. To enable these children to have the best life possible, their parents need to be able to cope. Emotional and practical support in the care for the child and other siblings along with good relationships with the healthcare providers can significantly improve the parents' ability to cope.

The children and their parents should be well informed about the condition and medics should listen to them to learn more about what it is like to live with chronic illness.

The normal process of parenting changes and develops over time in response to the development and growth of a child. Parenting a child with a chronic illness is no different in that it is an ongoing process, subject to change. Parents cope through managing the situation, addressing issues and problems, communicating their emotions, seeking information and accepting support.

Owen taught me how to parent to the best of my ability. He showed me how, in the face of adversity, to be brave and courageous and to strive to overcome what seem like insurmountable difficulties. Owen, Liam, Kate and I lived the research for this book. I hope Owen's experiences, good and bad, can illuminate the theory behind the strategies.

I can identify our particular coping strategy as being one of complete involvement. We tried to learn as much as possible about Owen's tumour and how his treatment affected him, physically and psychologically. We stayed with him during every procedure, every hospital stay and appointment; and we handed him over to the neurosurgeon asking that he look after him because we had simply never left him with anyone but the closest of friends and family. We questioned and challenged medics to the point of being irritating and demanding but knowing all the while that Owen's wellbeing was more important than upsetting those who should be professional enough to appreciate our concerns.

While we can question our choices regarding treatment, we know that we made the best decisions with the best information and advice we had at the time. We can take comfort in knowing that we did our utmost to care for Owen, even if it simply was not enough to keep him with us.

Sharon Dempsey can be contacted through her publishers at Jessica Kingsley Publishers, 116 Pentonville Road, London N1 9JB.

Contacts and Information Sources

UK

Action For Kids
www.actionforkids.org

Asthma UK
Summit House
70 Wilson Street
London EC2A 2DB
Tel: 020 7786 4900
Fax: 020 7256 6075
email: info@asthma.org.uk
website: www.asthma.org.uk

Cancer Index
www.cancerindex.org/ccw/guide2sg.htm

Cancerbackup
www.cancerbackup.org.uk/Cancertype/Childrenscancers/Organisations/
Suppliers

Children with Leukaemia
51 Great Ormond Street
London WC1N 3JQ
Tel: 020 7404 0808
Fax: 020 7404 3666
email: info@leukaemia.org
website: www.leukaemia.org

The Children's Society
www.childrenssociety.org.uk

Clic Sargent
Griffin House
161 Hammersmith Road
London W6 8SG
Tel: 020 8752 2800
Fax: 020 8752 2806
email: info@clicsargent.org.uk
website: www.clicsargent.org.uk

Coeliac UK
Suites A–D
Octagon Court
High Wycombe
Bucks HP11 2HS
Tel: 01494 437278
Fax: 01494 474349
website: www.coeliac.co.uk

Contact a Family
www.cafamily.org.uk

Council for Disabled Children
National Children's Bureau
8 Wakley Street
London EC1V 7QE
Tel: 020 7843 1900
Fax: 020 7843 6313
email: cdc@ncb.org.uk
website: www.ncb.org.uk

Cystic Fibrosis Trust
11 London Road
Bromley
Kent BR1 1BY
Tel: 020 8464 7211
Fax: 020 8313 0472
email: enquiries@cftrust.org.uk
website: www.cftrust.org.uk

Diabetes UK Central Office
Macleod House
10 Parkway
London NW1 7AA

Tel: 020 7424 1000
Fax: 020 7424 1001
email: info@diabetes.org.uk
website: www.diabetes.org.uk

Every Child Matters
www.everychildmatters.gov.uk/socialcare/disabledchildren

Family Fund
Unit 4
Alpha Court
Monks Cross Drive
Huntingdon
York YO32 9WN
Tel: 0845 130 4542
Fax: 01904 652625
email: info@familyfund.org.uk
website: www.familyfund.org.uk

I CAN
8 Wakley Street
London EC1V 7QE
Tel: 0845 225 4071
Fax: 0845 225 4072
email: info@ican.org.uk
website: www.ican.org.uk

Juvenile Diabetes Research Foundation Head Office
19 Angel Gate
City Road
London EC1V 2PT
Tel: 020 7713 2030
Fax: 020 7713 2031
email: info@jdrf.org.uk
website: www.jdrf.org.uk

National Eczema Society
Hill House
Highgate Hill
London N19 5NA
website: www.eczema.org

NHS Direct
Tel: 0845 4647
website: www.nhsdirect.co.uk

Shared Care Network
Units 63–66
Easton Business Centre
Felix Road
Bristol BS5 0HE
Tel: 0117 941 5361
Fax: 0117 941 5362
email: Shared-care@bristol.ac.uk
website: www.sharedcarenetwork.org.uk

Whizz-Kidz
Elliot House
10–12 Allington Street
London SW1E 5EH
Tel: 020 7233 6600
email: info@whizz-kidz.org.uk
website: www.whizz-kidz.org.uk

Ireland

The Barretstown Camp Fund Ltd
Barretstown Castle
Ballymore Eustace
Co. Kildare
Tel: 045 864115
Fax: 045 864197
website: www.barretstown.org

The Cystic Fibrosis Association of Ireland
CF House
24 Lower Rathmines Road
Dublin 6
Lo-call: 1890 311 211
Tel: 01 496 2433
Fax: 01 496 2201
email: info@cfireland.ie
website: www.cfireland.ie

USA

The American Lung Association
61 Broadway
6th Floor
New York
NY 10006
Tel: 212-315-8700
website: www.lungusa.org

Brave Kids
www.bravekids.org

Centers for Disease Control and Prevention
1600 Clifton Road
Atlanta
GA 30333
Tel: 498-1515
email: ccdinfo@cdc.gov
website: www.cdc.gov/nccdphp

Children with Diabetes
www.childrenwithdiabetes.com

Council for Children and Adolescents with Chronic Health Conditions
21 South Fruit Street
Suite 22
Concord
NH 03301
Tel: 603-225-6400
Fax: 603-271-1156
email: ccachc@conversent.net
website: www.ccachc.org

Hospital-based Online Pediatric Environment (HOPE)
www.hopeconnectskids.org

National Diabetes Education Program
One Diabetes Way
Bethesda
MD 20814-9692
Tel: 1-888-693-NDEP
email: ndep@mail.nih.gov
website: www.ndep.nih.gov

National Dissemination Center for Children with Disabilities
PO Box 1492
Washington DC 20013-1492
Toll-free: 1-800-695-0285
Tel: 202-884-8200
Fax: 202-884-8441
email: nichcy@aed.org
website: www.nichcy.org

National Kidney Foundation
30 East 33rd Street
Suite 1100
New York
NY 10016
Toll-free: 1-800-622-9010
Tel: 212-889-2210
Fax: 212-689-9261
website: www.kidney.org

Our-Kids
www.our-kids.org

Pacer
www.pacer.org

PADRE Foundation
455 South Main Street
Orange
CA 92868
Tel: 714-532-8330
Fax: 714-532-8398
website: www.padrefoundation.org

Starlight Starbright Children's Foundation
5757 Wilshire Boulevard
Suite M100
Los Angeles
CA 90036
Tel: 310-479-1212
Fax: 310-479-1235
email: info@starlight.org
website: www.starlight.org

Canada

Canadian Healthcare Association
17 York Street
Ottawa
Ontario
K1N 9J6
Tel: 613-241-8005
Fax: 613-241-5055
email: info@cha.ca
website: www.cha.ca

SickKids Foundation
525 University Avenue
14th Floor
Toronto
Ontario
M5G 2L3
Tel: 416-813-6166
Fax: 416-813-5024
email: donor.inquiries@sickkidsfoundation.com
website: www.sickkidsfoundation.com

References

Preface

1. Brain Tumour UK (n.d.) *Fighting Brian Tumours Together Through Research.* Accessed on 10 August 2007 at: www.braintumouruk.org.uk/research.htm

Chapter 1

1. Travis, G. (1976) *Chronic Illness in Children.* Stanford, CA: Stanford University Press.

2. Davis, H. (1993) *Counselling Parents of Children with Chronic Illness or Disability.* Leicester: BPS Books.

3. Melnyk, B.M., Feinstein, N.F., Moldenhouer, Z. and Small, L. (2001) 'Coping in parents of children who are chronically ill: strategies for assessment and intervention.' *Pediatric Nursing,* November–December. Accessed on 4 May 2007 at: http://findarticles.com/p/articles/mi_m0FSZ_is_6_27/ai_n18612858

4. Davis, H. (1993) *Counselling Parents of Children with Chronic Illness or Disability.* Leicester: BPS Books, p.82.

Chapter 2

1. Worchel, F.F., Copeland, D.R. and Barker, D.G. (1987) 'Control-related coping strategies in pediatric oncology patients.' *Journal of Pediatric Psychology 12,* 1, 25–38.

2. Jerram, H., Raeburn, J. and Stewart, A. (2005) 'The strong parents–strong children programme: parental support in serious and

chronic child illness.' *Journal of the New Zealand Medical Association 118*, 1224, 28 October. Accessed on 10 July 2007 at: www.nzma.org.nz/journal/118-1224/1700

3. Davis, H. (1993) *Counselling Parents of Children with Chronic Illness or Disability.* Leicester: BPS Books, p.53.

4. Hymovich, D.P. and Hagopian, G.A. (1992) *Chronic Illness in Children and Adults: Psychological Approach.* Philadelphia, PA: W.B. Saunders Company, pp.104–105.

5. Hymovich, D.P. and Hagopian, G.A. (1992) *Chronic Illness in Children and Adults: Psychological Approach.* Philadelphia, PA: W.B. Saunders Company, pp.50–51.

6. Hamers, J.P.H., Abu-Saad, H.H., van den Hout, M.A. and Halfens, R.J.G. (1998) 'Are children given insufficient pain-relieving medication postoperatively?' *Journal of Advanced Nursing 27*, 1, 37–44.

7. Stinson, J.N. and McGrath, P. (2007) 'No pain – all gain: advocating for improved paediatric pain management.' *Paediatric Child Health 12*, 2, 93–94.

8. Kain, Z.N., Mayes, L.C., Caldwell-Andrews, A.A., Karas, D.E. and McClain, B.C. (2006) 'Preoperative anxiety, postoperative pain, and behavioral recovery in young children undergoing surgery.' *Pediatrics 118*, 2, 651–658.

9. Hymovich, D.P. and Hagopian, G.A. (1992) *Chronic Illness in Children and Adults: A Psychological Approach.* Philadelphia, PA: W.B. Saunders Company, pp.50–51.

10. Dempsey, S. (2002) *My Brain Tumour Adventures.* London: Jessica Kingsley Publishers.

11. Hymovich, D.P. and Hagopian, G.A. (1992) *Chronic Illness in Children and Adults: A Psychological Approach.* Philadelphia, PA: W.B. Saunders Company, p.231.

12. Hinds, P.S., Drew, D., Oakes, L.L., Fouladi, M. *et al.* (2005) 'End-of-life care preferences of pediatric patients with cancer.' *Journal of Clinical Oncology 23*, 36, 9146–9154.

Chapter 3

1. Davis, H. (1993) *Counselling Parents of Children with Chronic Illness or Disability.* Leicester: BPS Books, p.22.

2. Perrin, E.C., Lewkowicz, C. and Young, M.H. (2000) 'Shared vision: concordance among fathers, mothers, and pediatricians about unmet needs of children with chronic health conditions.' *Pediatrics 105*, 1, Supplement, January, 277–285.

3. Davis, H. (1993) *Counselling Parents of Children with Chronic Illness or Disability.* Leicester: BPS Books.

4. Housden, M. (2002) *Hannah's Gift: Lessons from a Life Fully Lived.* London: Thorsons.

5. Perrin, E.C., Lewkowicz, C. and Young, M.H. (2000) 'Shared vision: concordance among fathers, mothers, and pediatricians about unmet needs of children with chronic health conditions.' *Pediatrics 105*, 1, Supplement, January, 277–285.

6. Davis, H. (1993) *Counselling Parents of Children with Chronic Illness or Disability.* Leicester: BPS Books, pp.78–79.

7. Davis, H. (1993) *Counselling Parents of Children with Chronic Illness or Disability.* Leicester: BPS Books, pp.114–115.

8. Travis, G. (1976) *Chronic Illness in Children.* Stanford, CA: Stanford University Press, pp.380–381.

9. Young, B., Dixon-Woods, M., Windridge, K.C. and Heney, D. (2003) 'Managing communication with young people who have a potentially life threatening chronic illness: qualitative study of patients and parents.' *BMJ 326*, 8 February, 305.

10. Beresford, B. (1999) *Identification of the Information Needs of Chronically Ill or Physically Disabled Children and Adolescents, and Development of Recommendations for Good Practice.* York: Social Policy Research Unit, University of York.

11. Scott, J.T., Harmsen, M., Prictor, M.J., Sowden, A.J. and Watt, I. (2001) 'Interventions for improving communication with children and adolescents about their cancer.' *Cochrane Database of Systematic Reviews*, Issue 1. Accessed on 8 November 2007 at: www.cochrane.org/reviews/en/ab002969.html

12. Hymovich, D.P. and Hagopian, G.A. (1992) *Chronic Illness in Children and Adults: A Psychological Approach.* Philadelphia, PA: W.B. Saunders Company, pp.159–160.

13. Travis, G. (1976) *Chronic Illness in Children.* Stanford, CA: Stanford University Press, p.387.

14. Sawyer, S.M. and Aroni, R.A. (2005) 'Self-management in adolescents with chronic illness. What does it mean and how can it be achieved?' *The Medical Journal of Australia.* Accessed on 16 August 2007 at: www.mja.com.au/public/issues/183_08_171005/saw10483_fm.html

Chapter 4

1. Davis, H. (1993) *Counselling Parents of Children with Chronic Illness or Disability.* Leicester: BPS Books.

2. Perrin, E.C., Lewkowicz, C. and Young, M.H. (2000) 'Shared vision: concordance among fathers, mothers, and pediatricians about unmet needs of children with chronic health conditions.' *Pediatrics 105,* 1, Supplement, January, 277–285.

3. Travis, G. (1976) *Chronic Illness in Children.* Stanford, CA: Stanford University Press.

4. Bauman, L.J., Drotar, D., Leventhal, J.M., Perrin, E.C. and Pless, I.B. (1997) 'A review of psychosocial interventions for children with chronic health conditions.' *Pediatrics 100,* 2, 244–251.

5. Davis, H. (1993) *Counselling Parents of Children with Chronic Illness or Disability.* Leicester: BPS Books, p.30.

6. Hymovich, D.P. and Hagopian, G.A. (1992) *Chronic Illness in Children and Adults: A Psychological Approach.* Philadelphia, PA: W.B. Saunders Company, p.215.

7. Neinstein, L.S. (2001) 'The treatment of adolescents with a chronic illness.' *Western Journal of Medicine 175,* November, 293–295.

8. Adams, R., Peveler, R.C., Stein, A. and Dunger, D.B. (1991) 'Siblings of children with diabetes: involvement, understanding and adaptation.' *Diabetic Medicine 8,* 855–859.

9. Feudtner, C., Haney, J. and Dimmers, M.A. (2003) 'Spiritual care needs of hospitalized children and their families: a national survey of pastoral care providers' perceptions.' *Pediatrics 111,* 1, January, e67–e72.

Chapter 5

1. Kliebenstein, M.A. and Broome, M.E. (2000) 'School re-entry for the child with chronic illness: parent and school personnel perceptions.' *Pediatric Nursing 26*, November, 579–582.

2. USA Today (Society for the Advancement of Education) (1993) 'Overprotectiveness should be avoided – care of chronically ill children.' Accessed on 19 August 2007 at: http://.findarticles.com/p/articles/mi_m1272/is_n2581_v122/ai_14236167

3. Bannon, M.J. and Ross, E.M. (1998) 'Administration of medicines in school: who is responsible?' *BMJ 316*, 23 May, 1591–1593.

4. Yude, C. and Goodman, R. (1999) 'Peer problems of 9- to 11-year-old children with hemiplegia in mainstream schools. Can these be predicted?' *Developmental Medicine and Child Neurology 41*, 1, January, 4–8.

5. Travis, G. (1976) *Chronic Illness in Children*. Stanford, CA: Stanford University Press, p.186.

6. Moynihan, P.M. and Haig, B. (1989) *Whole Parent Whole Child*. McLean, VA: DCI Publishing Inc.

7. Op. cit.

8. Kliebenstein, M.A. and Broome, M.E. (2000) 'School re-entry for the child with chronic illness: parent and school personnel perceptions.' *Pediatric Nursing 26*, November, 579–582.

9. Travis, G. (1976) *Chronic Illness in Children*. Stanford, CA: Stanford University Press, p.393.

Chapter 6

1. Galvin, E., Boyers, L., Schwartz, P.K., Jones, M.W. *et al.* (2000) 'Challenging the precepts of family-centered care: testing a philosophy.' *Pediatric Nursing*, November. Accessed on 8 August 2007 at: http://findarticles.com/p/articles/mi_m0FSZ/is_6_26/ai_n18611002/pg_1

2. Fegan, M.W. (1994) 'She doesn't look sick to me – caring for a chronically ill child.' *Vibrant Life*, March–April. Accessed on 25 November 2007 at: http://findarticles.com/p/articles/mi_m0826/is_n2_v10/ai_14942940

3. Sadovsky, R. (2005) 'Stress patterns in parents of chronically ill children.' *American Family Physician*, 15 August. Accessed on 13 November 2007 at: http://findarticles.com/p/articles/mi_m3225/is_4_72/ai_n15623964

4. Hymovich, D.P. and Hagopian, G.A. (1992) *Chronic Illness in Children and Adults: A Psychological Approach*. Philadelphia, PA: W.B. Saunders Company, p.185.

5. Worthington, R.C. (1989) 'The chronically ill child and recurring family grief.' *Journal of Family Practice*, October. Accessed on 10 April 2007 at: http://findarticles.com/p/articles/mi_m0689/is_n4_v29/ai_8138881

6. Neinstein, L.S. (2001) 'The treatment of adolescents with a chronic illness.' *Western Journal of Medicine 175*, November, 293–295.

Chapter 7

1. Black, D. (1998) 'The dying child.' *BMJ 316*, 2 May, 1376–1378.

2. Goodall, J. (1994) 'Care of the dying child.' *BMJ 309*, 12 November, 1311.

3. Goldman, A. (1998) 'ABC of palliative care: special problems of children.' *BMJ 316*, 3 January, 49–52.

4. Travis, G. (1976) *Chronic Illness in Children*. Stanford, CA: Stanford University Press, pp.398–399.

5. Surkan, P.J. (2006) 'Predictors and consequences of loss of a child: Nationalwide epidemiological studies from Sweden.' Dissertation. Föreläsningssalen, Cancer Centrum Karolinska Universitetssjukhuset, Solna, 15 December.

6. Beale, E.A., Baile, W.F. and Aaron, J. (2005) 'Silence is not golden: communicating with children dying from cancer.' *Journal of Clinical Oncology 23*, 15, 3629–3631.

7. Kreicbergs, U., Valdimarsdóttir, U., Onelöv, E., Henter, J.I. and Steineck, G. (2004) 'Talking about death with children who have severe malignant disease.' *New England Journal of Medicine 351*, 12, 1175–1186.

8. Black, D. (1998) 'The dying child.' *BMJ 316*, 2 May, 1376–1378.

9. Feudtner, C., Haney, J. and Dimmers, M.A. (2003) 'Spiritual care needs of hospitalized children and their families: a national survey of pastoral care providers' perceptions.' *Pediatrics 111*, 1, January, e67–e72.

Bibliography

Adams, R., Peveler, R.C., Stein, A. and Dunger, D.B. (1991) 'Siblings of children with diabetes: involvement, understanding and adaptation.' *Diabetic Medicine 8*, 855–859.

Barret Singer, A.T. (1999) *Coping with Your Child's Chronic Illness.* San Francisco, CA: Robert D. Reed Publishers.

Bauman, L.J., Drotar, D., Leventhal, J.M., Perrin, E.C. and Pless, I.B. (1997) 'A review of psychosocial interventions for children with chronic health conditions.' *Pediatrics 100*, 2, August, 244–251.

Beale, E.A., Baile, W.F. and Aaron, J. (2005) 'Silence is not golden: communicating with children dying from cancer.' *Journal of Clinical Oncology 23*, 15, 3629–3631.

Beresford, B. and Sloper, P. (1999) *The Information Needs of Chronically Ill or Physically Disabled Children and Adolescents.* York: Social Policy Research Unit, University of York. Accessed on 8 November 2007 at: www.york.ac.uk/inst/spru/pubs/pdf/infoneeds.pdf

Black, D. (1998) 'The dying child.' *BMJ 316*, 2 May, 1376–1378.

Committee on Pediatric AIDS (1999) 'Disclosure of illness status to children and adolescents with HIV infection.' *Pediatrics 103*, 1, January, 164–166.

Cooley, W.C. and Committee on Children with Disabilities (2004) 'Providing a primary care medical home for children and youth with cerebral palsy.' *Pediatrics 114*, 4, 1 October, 1106–1113.

Davis, H. (1993) *Counselling Parents of Children with Chronic Illness or Disability.* Leicester: BPS Books.

Ellis, R. and Leventhal, B. (1993) 'Information needs and decision-making preferences of children with cancer.' *Psycho-Oncology 2*, 277–284.

Farmer, E., Marien, W.E., Clark, M.J., Sherman, A. and Selva, T.J. (2004) 'Primary care supports for children with chronic health conditions: identifying and predicting unmet family needs.' *Journal of Pediatric Psychology 29*, 5, 1 July, 355–367.

Feudtner, C., Haney, J. and Dimmers, M.A. (2003) 'Spiritual care needs of hospitalized children and their families: a national survey of pastoral care providers' perceptions.' *Pediatrics 111*, 1, January, e67–e72.

Foreman, N.K., Faestel, P.M., Pearson, J., Disabato, J. *et al.* (1999) 'Health status in 52 long-term survivors of pediatric brain tumors.' *Journal of Neuro-Oncology 41*, 1, January, 47–53.

Hinds, P.S., Drew, D., Oakes, L.L., Fouladi, M., *et al.* (2005) 'End-of-life care preferences of pediatric patients with cancer.' *Journal of Clinical Oncology 23*, 36, 20 December, 9146–9154.

Housden, M. (2002) *Hannah's Gift: Lessons from a Life Fully Lived.* London: Thorsons.

Hymovich, D.P. and Hagopian, G.A. (1992) *Chronic Illness in Children and Adults: A Psychological Approach.* Philadelphia, PA: W.B. Saunders Company.

Jerram, H., Raeburn, J. and Stewart, A. (2005) 'The strong parents–strong children programme: parental support in serious and chronic child illness.' *Journal of New Zealand Medical Association 118*, 1224, 28 October. Accessed on 10 July at: www.lnzma.org.nz/journal/118-1224/1700

Kliebenstein, M.A. and Broome, M.E. (2000) 'School re-entry for the child with chronic illness: parent and school personnel perceptions.' *Pediatric Nursing 26*, November, 579–582.

Lavigne, J.V., Traisman, H.S., Marr, T.J. and Chasnoff, I.J. (1982) 'Parental perceptions of the psychological adjustment of children with diabetes and their siblings.' *Diabetes Care 5*, 4, 420–426.

Liptak, G., Orlando, M., Yingling, J., Theurer-Kaufman, K. *et al.* (2006) 'Satisfaction with primary health care received by families of children with developmental disabilities.' *Journal of Pediatric Health Care 20*, 4, 245–252.

Liptak, G.S. and Revell, G.M. (1989) 'Community physician's role in case management of children with chronic illnesses.' *Pediatrics 84*, 3 September, 465–471.

Matthews, J. and Matthews, J. (2006) *The Self Help Guide for Special Kids and Their Parents.* London: Jessica Kingsley Publishers.

Moynihan, P.M. and Haig, B. (1989) *Whole Parent Whole Child.* McLean, VA: DCI Publishing Inc.

Neinstein, L.S. (2001) 'The treatment of adolescents with a chronic illness.' *Western Journal of Medicine 175*, November, 293–295.

Newacheck, P.W., McManus, M.A. and Fox, H.B. (1991) 'Prevalence and impact of chronic illness among adolescents.' *Archives of Pediatric and Adolescent Medicine 145*, 12, December, 1367–1373.

Perrin, E.C., Lewkowicz, C. and Young, M.H. (2000) 'Shared vision: concordance among fathers, mothers, and pediatricians about unmet needs of children with chronic health conditions.' *Pediatrics 105*, 1, Supplement, January, 277–285.

Phipps, S. and Steele, R. (2002) 'Repressive adaptive style in children with chronic illness.' *Psychosomatic Medicine 64*, 34–42.

Pradeep, R., Pradham, P.V. and Shah, H. (2004) 'Psychopathology and coping in parents of chronically ill children.' *The Indian Journal of Pediatrics 71*, 8, 695–699.

Sadovsky, R. (2005) 'Stress patterns in parents of chronically ill children.' *American Family Physician*, 15 August. Accessed on 13 November 2007 at: http://findarticles.com/p/articles/mi_m3225/is_4_72/ai_n15623964

Sahler, O.J., Frager, G., Levetown, M., Cohn, F.G. *et al.* (2000) 'Medical education about end-of-life care in the pediatric setting: principles, challenges, and opportunities.' *Pediatrics 105*, 575–584.

Steele, R. and Davies, B. (2006) 'Impact on Parents: When a child has a progressive life-threatening illness.' *International Journal of Palliative Care 12*, 576–585.

Travis, G. (1976) *Chronic Illness in Children.* Stanford, CA: Stanford University Press.

USA Today (Society for the Advancement of Education) (1993) 'Overprotectiveness should be avoided – care of chronically ill children.' Accessed on 19 August 2007 at: www.findarticles.com/p/articles/mi_m1272/is_n2581_v122/ai_14236167

von Korff, M., Glasgow, R.E. and Sharpe, M. (2002) 'Organising care for chronic illness.' *BMJ 325*, 13 July, 92–94.

Weaver, A.J. and Flannelly, K.J. (2004) 'The role of religion/spirituality for cancer patients and their caregivers.' *Southern Medical Journal 97*, 12, 1210–1214.

Worchel, F.F., Copeland, D.R. and Barker, D.G. (1987) 'Control-related coping strategies in pediatric oncology patients.' *Journal of Pediatric Psychology 12*, 1, 25–38.

Worchel, F.F., Nolan, B.F., Wilson, V.L., Purser, J., Copeland, D.R. and Pfefferbaum, B. (1988) 'Assessment of depression in children with cancer.' *Journal of Pediatric Psychology 13*, 101–112.

Worthington, R.C. (1989) 'The chronically ill child and recurring family grief.' *Journal of Family Practice*, October. Accessed on 10 April 2007 at: http://findarticles.com/p/articles/mi_m0689/is_n4_v29/ai_8138881

Yeo, M. and Sawyer, S. (2005) 'ABC of adolescence: chronic illness and disability.' *BMJ 330*, 26 March, 721–723.

Young, B., Dixon-Woods, M., Windridge, K.C. and Heney, D. (2003) 'Managing communication with young people who have a potentially life threatening chronic illness: qualitative study of patients and parents.' *BMJ 326*, 8 February, 305.

Zeltzer, L.K. and Schlank, C.B. (2005) *Conquering Your Child's Chronic Pain.* New York, NY: HarperCollins.

Subject Index

Author Index